Selling REMODELING

9 Steps to Sales Success

Victoria L. Downing

Introduction by Linda W. Case

HOME BUILDER PRESS

Home Builder Press®
National Association of Home Builders
1201 15th Street, NW
Washington, DC 20005-2800

Selling Remodeling: 9 Steps to Sales Success

ISBN 0-86718-381-0

Printed in the United States of America.

**Library of Congress
Cataloging-in-Publication Data**

Downing, Victoria L.
    Selling remodeling : 9 steps to sales success / Victoria L. Downing : introduction by Linda W. Case.
        p. cm.
    Includes bibliographical references.
    ISBN 0-86718-381-0
        1. Construction industry—United States—Management.
2. Buildings—United States—Repair and reconstruction. 3. Sales manage-ment—United States. I. Title
HD9715.U52D68   1992
690'.068'8—dc20   92-33760
                                                                                        CIP

This publication is designed to provide accurate and authoritative infor-mation in regard to the subject matter covered. It is sold with the under-standing that the publisher is not engaged in rendering legal, accounting, or other professional service. If legal advice or other expert assistance is required, the services of a competent professional person should be sought.

—From a declaration of Principles jointly adopted by a Committee of the Ameri-can Bar Association and a Committee of Publishers and Associations.

For further information, please contact—

Home Builder Press®
National Association of Home Builders
1201 15th Street, NW
Washington, DC 20005-2802

11/92   Rand/Courier   3M

Contents

Figures

About the Author

Victoria L. Downing serves as sales and marketing director for Remodeling Consulting Services, in Silver Spring, Maryland, a company that specializes in providing strategic information for and about remodelers. Downing also serves as executive director of Remodelers Executive Roundtables, an advanced educational think tank for the professional remodeler developed by her associate, Linda W. Case.

Earlier as marketing project manager of Wolverine Technologies, a manufacturer of building products, she participated in the development of Wolverine's Professional Dealer Program. This program used videotapes and educational materials to teach lead generation and sales skills to Wolverine's contractor customers.

A former senior account executive for Bailey, Klepinger, Medrich, and Muhlberg, an advertising agency based in Ann Arbor, Michigan, Downing guided the implementation of extensive marketing programs for several national firms and organizations.

Downing serves on the Board of Directors of the National Association of the Remodeling Industry and is a member of the Education Committee of the NAHB Remodelors® Council. Her articles on marketing and sales have been published by the top magazines in the industry. In addition, she writes "Marketing in the 90s," a monthly column for *Remodeling News*, an East Coast trade publication.

Acknowledgments

Selling for Remodeling: 9 Steps to Sales Success is a compilation of the sales methods and techniques used by some of the best remodeling professionals in the business. Down to the last, all of them happily shared what some might think of as their most powerful sales secrets. These remodelers deserve a round of thanks from anyone who finds him- or herself closing additional sales at increased profits after reading this book.

I thank my associate, Linda W. Case, for sharing her knowledge of the industry and the ins and outs of writing a book. Her enthusiasm, encouragement, and advice made this project possible.

Special thanks go to reviewers Jonathan Wallick, CGR, president, Wallick Construction, New Orleans, Louisiana; Edward W. McGowan, CGR, president, McGowan Corporation, Binghamton, New York; Steve Zarndt, CGR, sales manager, J. J. Schwartz, Decatur, Illinois; and to the Publications Work Group of the NAHB Remodelors® Council's Education Committee: Group leader Jonathan Wallick; Eugene Peterson, president, First General Services, Midvale, Utah; and Tony Thompson, president, Services Unlimited, Columbia, South Carolina. Dawn Harris, director, NAHB Personnel Department, provided helpful suggestions for Chapter 10, Manage the Sales Function.

One of the most important people to me in the creation of a first book, has been my editor, Doris M. Tennyson, director, special projects/senior editor, NAHB Home Builder Press. Doris helped me develop a logical format for organizing the many views and ideas of selling and to turn this information into a flowing, easy-to-read information package. Her guidance also made the book-writing process less complicated and more fun. Thank you.

Victoria L. Downing

Book Preparation

This book was prepared under the general direction of Kent Colton, NAHB executive vice president, in association with NAHB staff members James E. Johnson, Jr., staff vice president, Operations and Information Services; Adrienne Ash, assistant staff vice president, Publishing Services; Rosanne O'Connor, director of publications; Doris M. Tennyson, director, special projects/ senior editor and project editor; Carolyn Poindexter, editorial assistant; and David Rhodes, art director.

Note

Because this book is directed primarily toward small-volume and medium-volume remodelers who do their own selling, the words *remodeler* and *remodeling salesperson* are sometimes used interchangeably but not when a distinction in their roles occurs.

Introduction

Why Write a Sales Book for Remodelers?

The 90s hold great promise and tremendous challenge for remodelers. They will be challenged to become increasingly professional in all aspects of the business—marketing, production, cost control, management, and selling. For those remodelers that do make those quantum leaps in improvement, the business will be stable and lucrative. Those that don't will become as outmoded as the antique handplane.

This book extends the remodelers short bookshelf another half inch. It covers a critical subject—professional selling. The remodeler may have entered this industry to build, build, build—but to build, we must first sell. Indeed to build well, we must sell well.

The ingredients of successful selling are many. The top remodeling salesperson will undoubtedly enjoy people in their many diversities. The current buzz word in the bestseller sales books is *relationship selling*. These relationships with people come naturally to remodelers who have purposely chosen a service (read people) business.

The outstanding remodeling salesperson will be a problem-solver extraordinaire. Sales books in all industries stress consultative selling—finding the client's need and devising the ingenious solution. What could be more to the remodeler's liking and talent than problem-solving.

So why write this book if the remodeler already has so much natural sales ability? Because the top salesperson must be a closer of sales—he or she must ask for the next step. If remodelers have an industry failing, it is that they want their customers to beg to sign the contract. Yet, we know that customers want to be led through the selling process by a professional. Even if they want the product and service, they want to be softly pushed to the next step.

Selling Remodeling: 9 Steps to Sales Success is a powerful book. Victoria Downing has made the complex sales process simple. She has interviewed top remodeling salespeople across the United States and included their philosophies, guidelines, and tips. The remodeler will find successful sales techniques distilled into a workable, ready-to-use system.

Read and study. Try out the ideas. Stay on the road of constant improvement. And watch sales soar!

—Linda W. Case, President
Remodeling Consulting Services
Silver Spring, Maryland

Chapter 1

Successful Selling

Selling is a vital part of a successful remodeling business. The salesperson feeds jobs into the company, creating work and income for all of the other employees. A healthy sales record is a key step to the profitable future of a remodeling company. Without steady sales, the company is in peril.

However, many remodelers look at selling as a necessary evil. They see it as a part of the business that must be dealt with in order to allow the remodeler to spend time doing what he or she really enjoys—improving and remodeling buildings. Some remodelers view selling as a series of manipulative tactics that will convince prospects to buy something that they may not really need. They consider selling techniques a bag of tricks to help pull the wool over the eyes of customers who are then enticed to sign a contract.

This way of selling goes against the grain of most remodelers who truly want to help the customer. Because some remodelers see selling as an undesirable way to make a living, they resist learning how to do it well. And this resistance may affect the company's ability to be as successful as possible.

The Changing Marketplace

Today, the way people sell products and services is changing. Much of this change results from the increasing awareness and sophistication of the consumer. The consumer of the 1990s is much more knowledgeable than ever before. Because prospects are increasingly savvy, the hard manipulative sell of the past is no longer effective.

Problem-Solvers

This change is great news for remodelers. They are moving far away from the reputation of the tin man to becoming an expert consultant on whom the consumers rely for educated, expert solutions to their remodeling problems.

Remodeling salespeople are becoming expert consultants on whom the consumers rely for creative, educated solutions to their remodeling problems.

They form long-term relationships with their clients that are much deeper and stronger than the surface contacts of the past when a remodeler would do one job for one client and not care about the future.

Many remodelers find this improved image of the salesperson as problem-solver more comfortable and adaptable to their personalities. Because they can see themselves in this role, more remodelers are finally realizing that improving sales skills promotes the overall success of the business.

The Selling Process

But before remodeling salespeople can be successful, they must understand the logical steps that constitute the sales process. Once this process is understood and incorporated into a comprehensive set of procedures, they will find themselves selling more effectively and enjoying it more.

The 9 main steps in the selling process are listed in Figure 1-1.

Build a Relationship

All of the steps mentioned in Figure 1-1 are stages in the relationship sale. In relationship selling, the successful remodeling salesperson cultivates a trusting alliance with clients that is the basis for a lifetime relationship. The salesperson knows that the first sale is only one step in a long-term, mutually beneficial business relationship. Once a customer has chosen a remodeling company, this client can be the source of years of repeat business and high-quality referral leads. But the client will provide this additional business only if a trusting rapport develops with the remodeler and the prospect truly believes that he or she has solved the remodeling problem innovatively.

> **Figure 1-1.**
> **Steps in the Selling Process**
>
> - Develop sales procedures
> - Qualify the prospect
> - Build rapport
> - Gather information
> - Present your company
> - Present solutions
> - Overcome objections
> - Ask for the order
> - Follow-up

But how does he or she create this rapport and trust with prospects? By really listening and treating each one like the most important person in the world. In too many sales presentations, the remodeling salesperson rushes through the interview period to spend much of the time talking about the benefits of the product or service.

In relationship selling, the remodeler puts the emphasis on listening and uncovering the true wants and needs of the prospect.

In relationship selling, the remodeler takes the opposite approach and puts the emphasis on listening. Today's successful remodeling salesperson decreases the product presentation, and expands the information-gathering section of the meeting to ask numerous, in-depth questions about the prospect's remodeling needs. People rarely buy actual products and services. Instead, the customers buy the benefits of those products and services—the way they make them feel better, make their lives easier or more fun. By asking in-depth questions, a remodeling salesperson can determine what a prospect really wants to gain. These questions serve two purposes.

First, the remodeling salesperson demonstrates real interest in the needs and wants of the homeowner. Second, the salesperson gathers facts that can make the difference in developing an ordinary or an extraordinary solution.

The nine steps in the sales process are discussed in the paragraphs that follow.

Develop a Successful Sales Procedure—As businesspeople, remodelers know that they cannot run their companies haphazardly. To be successful, a company needs structure and procedures that will help avoid problems and will ensure that all of the tasks are being handled—especially where a missed task could mean a lost sale.

Qualify and Sell Before the Appointment—Successful remodelers spend time at the beginning of a relationship to make sure that the lead warrants attention and can indeed turn into a profitable sale. Once this is determined, the company takes the opportunity to provide the prospect with information in advance of the first meeting.

Build Rapport—Presenting a friendly, professional image is crucial. The remodeling salesperson who wants to get off on the right foot will pay particular attention to this stage of the sales process. Because people prefer to buy from friends, the remodeling salesperson begins to develop this trusting friendship by showing a sincere interest in the lives of his or her prospects.

Gather Information—In order to create the best solution, the remodeler needs the right information. Therefore, gathering information is the most important part of the sales call. Well-thought out questions will encourage the prospect to talk and will draw out the essential details.

Present Your Company—While a remodeling salesperson can claim that his or her company is the best, hard evidence will confirm those statements. A professional presentation will demonstrate the reasons why one company is a better choice than another.

Present Solutions—After confirming the limits of the project, the remodeler is ready to show the prospect exactly how to solve the remodeling problem. If he or she has gathered the right information, the solution should perfectly fit the needs of the prospect.

Overcome Objections—Since most of the objections are dealt with during the course of the information-gathering stage, few should crop up at this point. However, several simple responses can help a remodeling salesperson effectively answer the prospect's concerns.

Ask for the Sale—A critical part of the remodeling salesperson's job is to ask for the business. This step should develop as a natural outgrowth of the process and should be a matter of simply moving forward.

Follow-Up After the Contract Is Signed—High-quality prospects are a source of business for years to come. Professional, courteous follow-up can ensure that the prospect will speak highly of the remodeling company to friends and neighbors.

Manage the Sales Function—At some point the remodeler may find that he or she needs an additional salesperson. When this situation occurs, the remodeler needs to find the right person and guide that new salesperson to success. The remodeler becomes a coach who motivates both him- or herself and the salesperson. The remodeler can use a variety of tools to help the salesforce achieve the company's goals.

Attract High-Quality Leads

Once a remodeler has incorporated the skills of the sales process, he or she still requires customers who need the company's services. A constant, comprehensive marketing and lead-generation plan is indispensable in supplying company leads. However, the quality of the leads generated can vary greatly. A remodeling salesperson can spend time with prospects who are overly price conscious and have no reason to favor one company over another. Or the salesperson can concentrate on high-quality leads—prospects referred by a previous client who know and appreciate the importance of high quality work, technical excellence, and superior customer service. Such prospects are interested in qualities other than just a low estimate, and thus price becomes a secondary issue. The successful remodeler knows that spending time with this group will provide highly profitable results.

How does a remodeler find high-quality prospects? Referral leads, the most desirable, come from many sources: previous customers, suppliers, real estate agents, community contacts, and many others. However, the most precious resource is previous, happy clients.

Because the previous customer has already worked with the remodeling company, and the experience was positive, a personal belief in that firm has developed. If the client was treated in a professional, courteous manner, the needs creatively met, and the final project satisfactorily delivered, these happy customers will be only too glad to spread the word. Wanting to talk about the

The successful remodeler knows that spending time with high-quality prospects will provide highly profitable results.

company that improved the client's home and lifestyle is human nature. When friends and neighbors work with the same company, it reinforces the fact that the latest customer made a wise decision.

Smart remodelers and remodeling salespeople plan for and encourage this response. They know that a homeowner who sees an addition built by a particular company—and hears the owner sing the praises of that company—is already partially sold on the company. This early selling makes the salesperson's job much easier.

Create an Active Referral Program

An active, consistent referral program can generate a wealth of referral leads. Regular contact is the key to keeping this valuable group thinking about the remodeling company. Maintaining a high level of awareness is necessary because the remodeling salesperson never knows when a previous customer has the opportunity to refer a possible client to the company.

Common courtesy, such as a "Thank you for your business" letter, a small gift at the end of a job, a request for a company evaluation, or recognition of the referrals sent your way, makes a positive impression and reinforces the professionalism of the remodeling firm. Considering the lack of customer service that is rampant in all service industries, this touch of politeness can make sure that the remodeling salesperson keeps that warm spot in the heart of a precious client.

Successful selling is the lifeblood of any remodeling company. The company may have the best quality workmanship in the business, but unless the remodeling salesperson (a) develops trusting relationships with his or her prospects and clients, (b) solves their remodeling problems effectively, and (c) encourages high-quality referral leads, the remodeling salesperson has little likelihood of ever having a chance to demonstrate the company's work.

Howard Goldstein, director of sales training, Sandler Sales Institute, in Rockville, Maryland, explains the situation this way," Salespeople have to learn to think of themselves as professionals, just like doctors or lawyers. And their roles are very similar, too. If you walked into the doctor's office with a sore elbow, he doesn't take one look, bring out an assortment of pills and ask you which one you want. No, he asks you a series of questions to help him find out what the real problem is. Only then will he offer you a solution to get rid of your pain.

"The salesperson has the same role with his or her prospects. Today's successful salesperson doesn't meet with a prospect and begin to pitch a product without knowing what is really causing the pain. Instead, he'll ask questions and find out, first, if he can help and only then (after gathering certain information) will he offer the solution that fits the needs of the prospects and takes away their pain."

Action Plan 1—Successful Selling

- Create a relationship with the prospect that will continue long past the initial sale.
- Create this relationship by emphasizing open-ended questions and listening carefully to your prospects' answers. They will provide the information you need to successfully close.
- Spend your time with high-quality prospects. You will find these prospects mainly through referrals—from friends of the company and happy, previous customers.
- Develop an active system to generate these high-quality leads. Regular contact, displays of appreciation for the business, and top-quality customer service will help you to generate these desirable leads.

Chapter 2

Developing Sales Procedures

Every time a prospect contacts a remodeling business, a certain amount of time is automatically dedicated to the prospective job. But the time spent on this initial contact is a fraction of the commitment that is made when the remodeler decides to actually meet with the prospect. Once a remodeling salesperson sets that appointment, 5 to 10 hours or more of valuable time has been committed to the particular project.

How the salesperson handles the start of the sales cycle—from the first contact to the appointment—can help him or her determine whether the lead is worth this significant investment.

Five Steps to a Successful Start

Determine Lead Quality—From the first telephone call the remodeling salesperson should begin gathering information that will reveal the quality of the lead.

Set Up the Appointment—The time of the meeting and having all potential decision-makers present can set a tone that will help the remodeling salesperson achieve his or her goals.

Sell the Prospect on the Company in Advance—Once the remodeling salesperson concludes that the prospect meets certain criteria and the job is worth an investment, he or she should begin the second step of selling the prospect on the abilities of the remodeling company. Advance selling can be as simple as a prearranged mailing that will reach the prospects before the initial meeting.

Plan for the Appointment—Successful remodeling salespeople set aside 15 minutes before each meeting to plan their meeting agenda and their goals for the first meeting. Advance planning can make the meeting run smoothly and help the salesperson reach his or her objectives for the meeting.

Practice Time Management—Remodelers build time management into every step and focus on the job at hand. They do not waste time on activities that are not directly associated with closing the sale. Remodelers need to make their selling time pay.

Qualify the Lead

The remodeling salesperson should start qualifying a prospect during the first telephone call. Some remodelers are so glad to get a telephone call from a prospect—any prospect—that they jump at the chance for work. Sometimes an overanxious salesperson will barely take the time to ask how the prospect heard about the company before scheduling an appointment.

But the successful remodeling salesperson knows that every time an appointment is made, he or she has set aside many hours of time. For each appointment the salesperson must plan for these time-consuming activities:

◆ preparation
◆ travel
◆ the actual appointment
◆ developing the estimate
◆ follow-up
◆ the second appointment with the prospect

Wise remodelers want to meet only with prospects who at least somewhat fit the profile of a desirable client. They do not want to waste time on those prospects that do not, either because of the scope of work, lack of budget, a personality clash, or the fact that the prospect is simply shopping for the lowest price available.

The first appointment is too late in the process for the remodeler to find out that the job is not right for the company. In this business the remodeling salesperson's most valuable commodity is time, and his time should be used to pursue those leads that are most likely to actually turn into profitable work for the company.

The remodeler will use the time much more effectively by spending half an hour to an hour with a prospect on the telephone up front instead of several hours at an appointment that is not going to produce a job. Yes, this means that the remodeler will turn down a small percentage of prospective work and offer it to other remodelers when appropriate.

Turning down prospective work can make some people rather nervous. But by being selective about the appointments accepted, they can spend their time more productively with prospects who will bring work to the firm. Calling on 10 unqualified leads takes the same amount of time as calling on 10 qualified leads. The difference is that the ratio of leads to sales is going to be much higher with the qualified leads. With such an easy way to increase a close ratio, a remodeler who does not qualify leads from the start is definitely missing an indispensable tool. "I'd say that we turn down 25 percent of the calls that come in," says Guy Semmes, president

Some remodelers are so glad to get a telephone call from a prospect—any prospect—that they jump at the chance for work.

In relationship selling, the remodeler puts the emphasis on listening and uncovering the true wants and needs of the prospect.

of Hopkins and Porter Construction, Inc., Potomac, Maryland. "But we always try to refer those prospects to someone else."

An in-depth conversation sprinkled with questions is a highly effective way for the remodeler to determine whether or not a caller is a high-quality lead. "We talk to prospects for up to 45 minutes," says Mark Goldsborough, president of Mitchell, Best, and Goldsborough, Rockville, Maryland. "By taking the time to qualify them on the phone, we can avoid wasting our time with an appointment."

In this initial conversation, the remodeler should look for several main qualifying clues:

◆ how the prospect came to call
◆ the type of job and its scope
◆ why the prospect is considering the project
◆ the prospect's budget range
◆ the level of research that the prospect has accomplished
◆ Why the prospect is considering the work

Sales Lead Form

Using a standard company lead form serves as a mental reminder to the remodeler or the person taking the call. This form helps to ensure that the remodeling salesperson (a) obtains immediately all of the essential information that qualifies the lead and (b) puts that information in writing for future reference.

Copies of the lead forms should be compiled into a master lead book—a binder to hold the information on all leads received by the company, their sources, and the results of each call. This information can be compiled regularly to show marketing trends as well as the success rate of each salesperson.

The lead form in Figure 2-1 uses a point system to rate the various leads for quality and feasibility.

Telephone Tips

A pleasant voice, polite tone, quick response, and prompt return of calls are a cornerstone of a professional phone technique. Many people are not aware that their voices can actually sound different when they are smiling from when they are frowning. A surly sounding employee is inexcusable. No one should be placed on hold for more than 30 seconds without someone checking on the caller and offering to take a message. Remodelers must regularly review their employees' telephone mannerisms and their own because bad habits can develop quickly.

An effective telephone style is even more important. If the prospective client does not think that his or her project is treated as important during this first conversation, convincing the him or her of that at the appointment will be much more difficult.

Figure 2-1. Sales Lead

Date _____

Name _____ Title _____

Street address _____

City, state, zip _____

Telephone: Home (_____) _____   Office (_____) _____

Type of Work (describe fully)— _____

_____

Reason for doing the Work— _____

Budget Range $_____ to $_____

Number of Points (Circle only one number in each section)

Type of Project
45—Room addition including kitchen, bath, and bedroom additions
35—Major remodeling that does not include an addition
25—Kitchen remodel
15—Bathroom remodel
10—Siding, windows, roof
 5—Small projects—porch, deck, etc.
_____ Total points

Personal Evaluation of prospect
20—Excellent
10—Average
 0—Poor
_____Total points

_____**Grand total points**

How did you hear of our company?
45—Repeat customer referral from previous customer, or referral from a friend of the company.
Who? _____
35—Received job site marketing piece, direct mail, phone call, or saw job site sign.
(Where? _____)
30—Attended open house.
25—Received direct mail piece.
20—Saw company advertisement.
Which one? _____
10—Visited booth at trade show.
Which show?_____
 0—Chose name from *Yellow Pages*.
 0—Other
_____ Total points

Comments _____

_____

Appointment set for _____

Result _____

Salesperson _____

Source: Reprinted with permission of Remodeling Consulting Services.

Having this chance to casually discuss the project also helps the prospect get to know the remodeler. Establishing rapport is the first step in building a trusting relationship. For this reason the person who qualifies the prospect on the telephone should be the same person who will keep the appointment. If another company employee schedules the appointments, the remodeling salesperson misses a significant opportunity to begin to build trust with a potential customer. People buy from people with whom they feel comfortable, and this first call is the beginning of this crucial compatibility.

Does the Job Fit?

If the remodeling company specializes in custom additions and the prospect wants a small bathroom update, the job may not be worth the investment to go through a detailed estimate and develop a full set of design drawings. The profit margin may not be high enough to justify this heavy allocation of time.

In fat times remodelers may have few qualms about referring this marginally profitable work to other companies. But in lean times most remodeling companies are hungry and are much more willing to take this work. To ensure that this smaller job is still profitable, the remodeling company usually must develop a more basic approach for this type of job, such as perhaps skipping the design sketches or simplifying the estimate. Remodelers should dedicate fewer hours to the job but still maintain high quality to maintain profitability.

No matter what the size or scope of a job, the remodeler has to look carefully at every lead before turning it down. "You have to realize that you're not going to sign every [prospective] client," says Larry Parrish, president of R. C. Parrish and Company, Inc., in Boulder, Colorado. "This takes the pressure off of forcing a match with prospects that just aren't suited to your company. If you ignore the signals and force a match, I'll guarantee that the job will turn out to be a problem."

What Quality Is the Lead?

A remodeling salesperson has a much higher likelihood of closing a referral lead than closing a sale with a prospect who found the company through the Yellow Pages.

Finding out how the prospect came to call this particular remodeling company tells a remodeler what marketing activities produce the most productive leads. A remodeling salesperson has a much higher likelihood of closing a referral lead than closing a sale with a prospect who found the remodeler's name through the *Yellow Pages*. Therefore, a remodeler often is willing to invest the time in a referral lead even when it may not fit well into the company's niche. Chances are that a small amount of time can capture the business, which makes it attractive.

If the prospect calling is from a source other than a referral (such as an advertisement), qualifying the lead should go even higher on the list of priorities. This prospective client may have called several other remodelers to bid on the same project, and he or she is likely to look at price as a primary reason to choose a particular company. The remodeling salesperson can still sell the job. But a lower quality lead may mean that the remodeler will have to structure the sales presentation differently in order to walk out with the business. Such leads may be a much harder sale.

Bring Up the Budget

Knowing whether or not a prospect has a realistic idea of a project's budget requirements is a key to a successful sale. Many remodelers fear asking the simple question, "Do you have a budget range in mind?" Since many customers do not have a clue as to what a high-quality remodeling job costs, the prospect's estimate is likely to be off target. If this problem arises, the remodeler can let the prospect know during this first contact that he or she may need to adjust the proposed budget.

Knowing whether or not a prospect has a realistic idea of a project's budget requirements is a key to a successful sale.

If the remodeler suggests the high and the low figures for an estimated budget for the job, the prospective customer will readily know whether he or she has planned for sufficient money. If the prospect has not allocated adequate funds, the remodeler can continue the conversation to determine whether the prospect can raise the budget to realistic levels. If the prospect will not increase the budget, reduce his or her expectations, or accept the remodeler's educated opinion on the projected costs, the remodeler has to face facts and realize that the time spent in this meeting may be wasted. However, a resourceful remodeler will have numerous alternatives available that may wonderfully meet the needs of the prospect at less expense.

A remodeler might think "If I go out there and meet the prospects, maybe I can convince them to spend the money they need to do the job right." But if the prospect wants to do a job for $8,000 and the remodeler knows that doing the basics right will take a minimum of $12,000, what is the benefit in discovering this fact at the first meeting (after the remodeler has invested several hours) instead of learning about it during the first telephone call? The professional remodeling salesperson would rather know in advance (a) if the prospects are prepared to make the necessary investment to do their projects right and to provide for a fair profit margin or (b) at least have an idea of how to work around this limitation.

How Much Do They Know?

"In order to find out if they have a realistic budget in mind, we ask them quite a few questions about where they are now in the education cycle," says Jack Hertig, president of Hertig Builders and Remodelers, Inc., Elkhart, Indiana. "We always ask them who they've discussed their project with even if it's just their brother-in-law. We also ask where they get their remodeling ideas, if they read shelter magazines or have seen other projects. If they have no idea of their budget range and are starting from scratch, we suggest they visit a couple of showrooms to begin to get an idea of what things cost. This way we won't waste time meeting with people who aren't serious about investing in their homes."

Mark Richardson, vice-president of Case Remodeling, Inc., Bethesda, Maryland, says, "I'll go on any call if I estimate that I have at least a 30 percent chance of closing the sale." So while the lead may not exactly fit the preferred prospective client profile, the remodeler should not be too quick to give it away.

Learn About the Prospect

In addition to getting the answers to the four important qualification questions, the remodeler can learn a great deal more about the prospect through this initial telephone conversation. Interesting facts about his or her life will come up naturally throughout the conversation. The more knowledge the remodeler has about the prospect, the easier it will be to meet the prospect's needs and find the right solution to the his or her problem.

Remodelers will want to take notes on the conversation and record the information listed below to use to create just the right presentation. If other decision-makers are involved, remodelers also need to obtain and use the appropriate information for that person or persons in the presentation:

◆ where the prospect works
◆ the approximate ages of members of the household
◆ how long the building has been owned
◆ whether the prospect has owned any other homes or other buildings
◆ the hobbies and group affiliations of the prospect
◆ what the prospect wants to accomplish with the proposed remodeling project
◆ whether other decision-makers are involved

Set Up the Appointment

In addition to being responsible for qualifying, the remodeling salesperson must make sure that all of the elements for a successful sale will be in place during the appointment.

Determine the Decision-Maker(s)

If a professional remodeler or remodeling salesperson is to have any possibility of closing the sale, the decision maker(s) must be present and ready to discuss the project. This question should help reveal the decision-maker: "If you like the ideas we discuss, will you feel comfortable making a decision to go ahead or do you need to consult someone else?"

The answer to this question will let the remodeler or remodeling salesperson know if another person should be present at the meeting. If the prospect admits that another person would have a say in the final decision, the remodeling salesperson would ask that this other person be present. If the prospect is a homeowner who would have to consult with a spouse, the response might be, "When you're remodeling your home, it has to be designed to meet all of your needs. You have to answer a lot of questions and make a lot of decisions before I can develop the right solutions. The process would be much clearer and easier for you if I could meet with you both. Could your spouse or the other owner(s) join us?" A similar approach could be used for any project.

If two homeowners are involved and one person has difficulty making an appointment during regular working hours, the remodeler should suggest alternative times that would be convenient for all parties. No one can present the remodeling company as well as the remodeler. If the remodeler meets with only one part of the decision-making team, he or she is allowing one prospect to present the company to the other decision-maker.

This prospect cannot possibly remember all of the details that make a particular company the best choice, so the other decision-maker will hear only part of the story. In that situation, a decision in the company's favor is doubtful. Selling is harder if the remodeling salesperson is unable to present the company and its professional expertise to all of the decision-makers.

When to Make the Appointment

Many remodeling salespeople will only make appointments for regular business hours. While they might arrange to meet with prospects as early as 7 a.m. or as late as 6 p.m. to provide as much convenience for the prospect as possible, as a rule remodelers or remodeling salespeople will not schedule evening or weekend appointments. Insisting on regular working hours demonstrates that remodelers and remodeling salespeople are professionals just like doctors or accountants. This practice intimates that the remodeling salesperson's time is valuable too.

"I try not to meet with prospects in the evenings or on the weekend," says Guy Semmes, president of Hopkins and Porter Construction, Inc., Potomac, Maryland. "If all of the decision makers can't meet during the working day, I'll suggest lunch hours, early morning or late afternoon meetings to make it as convenient as possible."

By taking time from work to meet the remodeler, the prospect invests in the project. If the prospect is not willing to rearrange a schedule, the commitment to the remodeling project may be too low to complete the sale. Lack of commitment means an unqualified lead. Jack Hertig, president of Hertig Builders and Remodelers, Inc., Elkhart, Indiana, says, "When prospects take time off from work to meet me and talk about their project, they've already given something. If they're not willing to take time off to meet with me, then their project must not be very important yet, and they're not ready to invest in it."

Larry Parrish adds, "The prospects' degree of flexibility in meeting with me is also a good indicator of how easy or difficult they will be to work with throughout their project. If they're willing to adjust their schedules, which shows that they're serious about their project, chances are that they'll be flexible in other areas which will make the project go much smoother. If a prospect just won't bend on this issue, it shows me that this prospect will be a difficult client, and I'll adjust accordingly."

If the prospect is meeting with salespersons from several firms, the wise remodeler arranges to be the last appointment because what the prospect saw and heard last is likely to be remembered longer.

Give the Prospect Homework

Many times, the prospect has to provide the remodeler with specific information such as a survey or zoning plan before a solution can be created. Asking the prospect to have this information ready for the appointment heads off a possible snag in the sales process. If the prospect is not informed that this information will be needed before the appointment, he or she will probably need several days to gather it. Enthusiasm for the project can cool off during this period. Investing the time to obtain such information before the first appointment also helps the prospect to commit to the project itself.

Many remodelers or remodeling salespeople ask their prospects to complete a few small tasks before their initial meeting. "I always ask my prospective clients to have a prioritized wish list ready," says Tim Wallace, president of T. W. Wallace Construction, Inc., in Arlington, Virginia. "This makes them clearly think out their real needs." Other tasks might include visiting showrooms to get ideas for tile, appliances, or cabinetry. Some remodelers will send a questionnaire to be completed and ready for discussion at the first meeting.

Sell the Company in Advance

After the remodeler or remodeling salesperson qualifies the lead and decides to make the investment in the potential job, he or she must begin selling the prospect on the attributes of the company. Since several days will usually pass between the initial telephone call and the actual appointment, the savvy remodeler or remodeling salesperson uses this time to illustrate professionalism with an informal contact. This contact typically includes a letter confirming the appointment and a packet of company information. This information may include a brief history of the company, the company's service philosophy, and the qualifications of the primary personnel. It may also include copies of articles that might have been written about the company or testimonial letters from satisfied customers.

The remodeler should develop one standard packet and write one basic letter that can be quickly personalized for each prospect. Writing a separate letter each time can waste time and could cause this important opportunity to slip away.

"We schedule our appointments at least one week after the initial call," says Mark Bartlett, vice president of River Crest Design Build, Annapolis, Maryland. "This gives us time for at least two mail contacts before we actually meet with them. The first is a thank you and confirmation letter, and the second is a brochure explaining the design build concept. We feel that this builds continuity, shows that we're professional and that we follow through."

By standardizing this follow-up, anyone in the office can handle it. The pieces will be ready to go into the mail before each appointment and will be easy to send out in minutes. This preappointment selling contact becomes another part of the total process that starts working with every new lead. With this reappointment packet, the remodeling company has informed the prospect that it is expert in the business and that previous customers think highly of the company's work. This packet prepares the prospect to meet a professional.

Plan for the Appointment

Thorough preparation demonstrates the skills of the successful remodeler. Not only does it impress the prospective customer but preparation gives the remodeler essential information that he or she needs to reach the goals of the sales call. In his book, *How to Master the Art of Selling,*® sales expert Tom Hopkins states that champion salespeople spend about 50 percent of their time in the essential areas of qualification and planning.[1] This attention to detail shows the prospect that the remodeling salesperson took the time to research the project. Extra attention goes a long way in raising the customer's estimation of the remodeling salesperson.

Many activities help a remodeling salesperson prepare for a sales call:

Champion salespeople spend about 50 percent of their time in the essential areas of qualification and planning.[1]

—Tom Hopkins
Sales Expert and Author
Scottsdale, Arizona

◆ Customize the presentation book to show finished projects that are similar to the prospect's proposed job. (For example, if the he or she is interested in bathrooms, the presentation book would include information and photos of several bathroom projects.)

◆ Gather into a leave-behind packet the manufacturers' product literature that displays the products the remodeler uses.

- Compile names of previous clients in the neighborhood into an impressive reference list.
- Drive through the neighborhood to get an idea of styles and ages of homes, and the lifestyles and income ranges of the residents. David Merrill, president of Merrill Contracting and Remodeling, Inc., Arlington, Virginia, says, "If I'm not familiar with the neighborhood, I'll take the time to drive through. This gives me an idea of what has been done to the other homes in the area and what their home might support."
- Look up typical prices in the newspapers for homes in the neighborhood. Again, this information will help the remodeling salesperson hone the presentation and fit the recommendations to what the prospect can afford to invest.
- If possible, find out the benefits and features of housing currently selling in the neighborhood. Determine which of these benefits and features the potential client's house lacks.

Develop an Agenda

Before a sales call, a remodeler asks him- or herself the questions listed below. Someone who is just beginning to sell remodeling would profit from using this set of questions as an exercise before each presentation. By writing down the answers to these questions, he or she will develop a logical agenda for gaining and giving information throughout the presentation. Those salespeople with more experience can use the questions to review and further sharpen their skills:

- Why should the prospect choose my company? Why are we the best?
- What can I offer to the prospect that my competition cannot?
- What do I want the prospect to remember?
- How will I demonstrate the benefits that my company offers?
- Why should the prospect act now?
- What backup information will convince them to act now?
- What will be the result of this sales call if it is successful?

Mark Goldsborough says, "Everybody should know the answers to these questions, but often we'll forget how to answer them smoothly and without hesitation. So we practice the answers until we come up with one that everyone agrees with. Then we'll type it up and distribute the list to all of the salespeople. This [procedure] makes sure that we're all prepared with the best response."

Each salesperson will cultivate a personal method for appointment-handling that fits his or her personality. But preparing an agenda before the presentation will help the salesperson stay organized and make the presentation complete.

Practice Time Management

Because the remodeler has a limited number of hours to devote to sales, effective time management is a must. The successful ones allocate their time in proportion to the goals they would like to achieve. They use prime business time for face-to-face sales as often as possible. They save appointment scheduling, paperwork, and administrative work for less valuable periods of the working day.

Organized records help the remodeler make as much from his or her office time as possible. He or she records each lead on a comprehensive lead form with space for all of the information gathered during all contacts with the prospect. The lead information should include the information in the following paragraphs (Figure 2-2).

Name(s) of the Decision-Makers—The correct spelling should be confirmed as this record will be the basis for all future correspondence.

Location of the Project—The remodeler should take location into consideration when planning the sales day. Successful remodeling salespeople consider driving time wasted and try to consolidate all of their appointments in one general area.

Directions—Having accurate directions saves a great deal of time and helps the remodeling salesperson to avoid getting lost and arriving late for an appointment.

Type of Project—This information allows the presentation materials to focus on the specific category of project.

Source—How did the prospect come to call the company? As mentioned earlier, the quality of the lead often depends on how the lead was initially generated.

Once the remodeling salesperson decides to move ahead with a prospect's project, he or she should create an individual file containing all of the pertinent details about the job. Ideally, the remodeler or remodeling salesperson should work on one project at a time, but often this approach is unrealistic. However, by grouping the information on each job in one place, he or she will not waste time searching for information. This simple system can make designing and estimating quicker and easier.

The remodeler should develop the habit of calling ahead to confirm all meetings. This practice saves time by making sure that everything is still on schedule. If not, the remodeler can use the time to work on another priority item.

A calendar large enough for notes and logging appointments or a time-management system is one of the most useful tools for the remodeling salesperson who wants to use his or her time to the fullest. Such a tool can guide the structuring of the sales day. It provides a convenient place to document all of the tasks that must

Figure 2-2. Qualifying Questions for the Phone Inquiry

[The following typical script is for qualifying leads on the telephone. While this script may require the remodeler to spend 20 minutes or more on the telephone, the information gathered will be invaluable when the remodeler is deciding if the lead is worth a further investment of time. After creating a script appropriate for his or her own company, a remodeler might want to create a form based on that script to facilitate capturing the information from the conversation.]

Thank you for calling [name of company].

How did you happen to learn about our company?

Ms., Mrs, Miss, or Mr. [caller's name], if you have a few minutes now to discuss your project I could be more helpful at our first meeting. If this time is not convenient, would you suggest a better time to call back?

Could you share with me what you are thinking about doing?

Do you have any pictures of the styles or items you like?

What . . . [do] you like best about your home?

Why do you want to do this project?

What would you like to accomplish at our first meeting?

Have you established an investment amount for this project? [If so, what is it?]

When would you hope to be able to use the new [addition, kitchen, etc.]?

Do you know we are an architectural design and a construction company?

If I'm able to meet your needs, would you be able to make a decision to proceed when we meet?

Will anyone else besides you . . . be involved in the decision? [If so, who?]

[If the lead does not fit your company's niche, you might use this script.]
We are a small company and involve ourselves in a limited number of projects each year. Each project we do must fit what we do best. While this project does not fit our business, perhaps we could recommend another company that you might want to call. Or I could have [insert name] from the company call you.

You mentioned price. What price range are you considering?

From what you have described, I do not think we can meet your needs. Perhaps you would like to talk with some other companies who are more suitable for your job.

Before we finish could I just confirm your name and address?

Source: Adapted from a script provided by Ted Brown, Traditional Concepts, Lake Bluff, Illinois

be done during any day or week. But to make the calendar work, the remodeling salesperson must refer to it regularly.

Selling is a percentage business, so the more sales calls the remodeler makes, the more sales he or she will close. But organization and efficiency are keys to handling a large volume.

Make Selling Time Pay

Basic math shows making an appointment with every prospect who calls can lose quite a bit of money for the company. For example, a remodeling company with a goal of $300,000 yearly volume has specific needs. The primary salesperson is probably the remodeler-owner who also wears the hat of the administrator, material-ordering person, and production supervisor. These roles may leave a fourth of the owner's total yearly work hours dedicated to selling.

By working a 50-hour week for 50 weeks a year, the remodeler will have approximately 625 hours of selling time available. Dividing the selling time into the amount of dollars that must be produced ($300,000) shows that each hour invested in a potential sale should produce a minimum of $480.

But considering that an average remodeling salesperson will close only 25 to 30 percent of the leads, the remodeler can easily see that the jobs they do get must produce three to four times this amount. If the remodeler plans to invest 8 hours of time working on a potential project, he or she needs to know that the job will produce at least $11,520 in volume. If the job is unlikely to support this volume, the remodeler might decide that the project may not be worth the effort.

Some remodelers think that they can save the company money by pounding nails on the job instead of selling. This idea is a fallacy.

Another remodeling company may have a full-time salesperson. This remodeling salesperson may work the same total number of hours as the remodeler-owner but is able to use all of this time for selling. An average remodeling salesperson is expected to generate $600,000 in volume for his or her company. Dividing this volume by the 2,000 total hours available (40 hours per week multiplied by 50 weeks per year) shows that the full-time remodeling salesperson must generate $300 per hour to reach the sales goals. Some remodeling salespeople work 50 hours a week, in which case they would need to generate $240 per hour. But again the remodeler must keep in mind that the firm will actually sell only a small percentage of the potential projects it develops.

A salesperson's greatest resource is time. However, time also is a limited resource so the remodeler must spend his or her time on the tasks that will produce the greatest outcome for the company.

Action Plan 2—Sales Procedures

- Take the time to talk to the prospect and ask questions at the beginning of the sales cycle—especially during the first telephone call—to determine the quality of a prospective buyer.
- Remember that each time you make an appointment, you are dedicating hours to a prospect who may or may not buy. Choosing to spend time with qualified prospects will provide greater dividends to the company.
- In addition to qualifying the prospect, determine whether the job fits the your company's niche.
- Inquire about the prospect's budget range during this first contact.
- Use professional telephone manners to create a professional image.
- Make sure all decision-makers are present at the first meeting if at all possible.
- Always check whether the prospect is talking to other companies. If so, you should make every attempt to be the last person to meet with the homeowner.
- Give the prospect a task to complete before the appointment to encourage him or her to become emotionally involved early in the process.
- If time permits, precede the appointment with a confirmation letter. This letter allows the prospect to become more familiar with the company.
- Determine your goals for the first meeting and plan an agenda to accomplish them.
- Sell during peak selling hours. Do paperwork during less productive times.

Chapter 3

Build Rapport

Appearances tell a story. If a man was wearing work clothes, carrying a trowel and was walking in a garden, someone might assume that this man was a gardener. But this assumption would not necessarily be true. In actuality, this person could be a wealthy homeowner who happened to enjoy gardening in his spare time, a horticulture professor doing research, or an author of fine garden books. But the clothes he wore told another story to the average passerby.

Put on Your Best Face

Set the Tone

The first impression the prospect receives will set the tone for the entire sales call.

The same principles apply to the impression a remodeler gives walking in the prospect's door. The way this remodeling salesperson is dressed will instantly convey a particular image to the prospect, not only of that person but also of the remodeling company. The first impression the prospect receives will set the tone for the entire sales call. In order to get a fresh perspective of the effect on prospective clients, the salesperson should mentally review the way he or she looks on a typical sales call.

Does the remodeling salesperson look like an experienced professional? What is he or she wearing? A freshly pressed sport coat and trousers with pressed shirt and tie or soiled jeans, a wrinkled workshirt, and a manufacturer's baseball hat? A neat, attractive skirt and blouse or faded jeans and a sweater? Are fingernails clean, neat, and trimmed or caked with dirt after a day on the job? Is hair combed and well-kept, or is it greasy and in need of a trim? Is the vehicle immaculate and well-kept, or is it filthy and filled with trash and debris? Is the company's presentation material neat and clean, or has it been pulled, wrinkled, from the bottom of a scratched briefcase?

Guy Semmes, president of Hopkins and Porter Construction, Inc., Potomac, Maryland, says, "I play it safe and wear khaki trousers, button-down shirt, jacket, and tie. It's professional but not too overdone."

Each detail of the remodeler's personal presentation can add to or detract from the overall effect. Especially today, when the majority of consumers have become suspicious of the honesty of service providers, anything that the remodeler can do to create an attitude of trust and comfort will help generate business for the company.

In addition to encouraging the prospect to feel relaxed and assured, the way the remodeling salesperson presents him- or herself is a direct implication of the way the company does business. If the salesperson has taken care of his or her appearance, the homeowner will feel more confident that this company will take the same care with the prospect's project, regardless of whether it is for a home or a business.

Some remodelers believe meeting prospects in work clothes is perfectly fine. "The prospect likes to know that you know your way around the job," these remodelers say. But top professionals agree that to show respect for the client, to increase credibility, to become established as an experienced professional businessperson, a remodeler's attire should err on the side of professionalism.

One of the best reasons to dress in a professional manner is that of economics. Many remodeling salespeople have found that because they are dressed as a professional, they are perceived as a true authority. This perception allows them to command higher prices and helps them to avoid the price competition that many are forced to face. "As soon as I took off my coveralls and dressed up to khakis and a company shirt, I could see the difference," says Lynn Bicknell of Bicknell Painting, Inc., in Fairfax, Virginia. "The price objections dropped considerably."

If a remodeler looks like a carpenter, the prospect may only be willing to pay carpenter's wages. But if he or she looks like a businessperson, the prospect is more likely to pay the prices that cover the overhead that goes with a legitimate business.

However, remodelers and remodeling salespersons should not go on calls dressed exclusively in expensive suits. Instead, they should follow local custom and dress on the same level as the people they are meeting. So if a remodeler's target market is lower- to middle-income homeowners, an expensive suit would be overdressing. In this case, a remodeler might choose to wear a nice jacket, sport shirt, tie, and slacks or a skirt and sweater instead of the formality of a suit. But if doctors, lawyers, and stockbrokers comprise the target market, a suit could be the perfect thing.

A rule of thumb for selling remodeling is to wear what will make the prospect feel comfortable and able to relate to the person doing the selling. A soothing first impression creates the overall tone for the remainder of the sales call.

Meet and Greet the Prospect

The first few minutes of a sales call are critical. At this point the remodeling salesperson begins to build the trusting relationship that will be the basis of the entire working relationship.

Politeness and courtesy are mainstays of any meeting with any prospect. Even before the remodeler gets to the door, this philosophy will stand out in these actions:

◆ Show respect for the prospect's home or office.
◆ Be careful in parking, do not block others.
◆ Use the sidewalk rather than walk across the lawn.
◆ Be sure to speak respectfully to the children playing in the yard.

This respect and courtesy may be noticed and appreciated by the prospect. Again, these small details show professionalism and help the remodeler stand out, especially because it is so lacking within most customer service industries. "Once or twice I made the mistake of parking in the drive and then had to go out to move the car when someone wanted in or out," says Jack Hertig, president of Hertig Builders and Remodelers, Inc., Elkhart, Indiana. "Now that I park in the street, I've discovered another benefit. I have much more time to observe the area and the house. This [observation] gives me a lot of information about the owners."

When greeting the prospect, the remodeler should begin by introducing him- or herself and the company by handing the prospect a business card and thanking the prospect again for the meeting. The remodeler should approach softly and with a nonthreatening manner. Direct eye contact and a sincere smile are comfortable habits to get into.

Politeness and courtesy are mainstays of any meeting with any prospect.

Help Prospects Feel Special

Nearly everyone knows at least one person with whom they always feel comfortable. This skill of putting people at ease is important both in business and personal relationships. These people consciously or intuitively know one important fact: most people feel special when they are asked to talk about themselves. And the person who encourages them to talk by asking truly interested questions will usually make a strong positive impression. This person will be remembered.

Many times the person answering the questions will not be able to pinpoint why they liked this special person so much. They just know that they felt good.

This skill should be learned and cultivated because a major goal of the remodeling salesperson is to allow the prospect to relax, which the prospect is not likely to do if he or she is afraid of getting a hard sell. If the prospect puts up defenses because the remodeling salesperson came on too strong or did not bother to build this crucial rapport, uncovering the information needed will be twice as difficult.

Building rapport with prospects is as simple as communicat-

This part of the sales call is building a relationship. A trusting, friendly approach will get the best response.

—Phil Rea, President
Phil Rea, Inc.
Newport News, Virginia

ing a genuine interest in them and their projects. The remodeler who communicates this interest to the prospects will be the person who gets the job. The professional knows that customers buy the salesperson first and the product second. Phil Rea, president of Phil Rea, Inc., Newport News, Virginia, thinks that building rapport is one of the most important parts of the sales call.

The best way to develop rapport comes from noticing and asking thoughtful questions about the prospect's environment, the household or something special in the home. Questions about the fishing rods in the hallway, the hunting trophy on the office wall, or the arrangement of children's photos will get the prospect talking about an aspect of their lives that is interesting to them. "We always ask them small questions just to get them talking," says Rea. "Questions about their kids and where they go to school shows interest but is very nonthreatening."

However, to be effective the remodeling salesperson must truly care. This caring cannot be faked because, if it is, the prospects will quickly know and consider the salesperson a phony from that minute on.

A remodeler must show enthusiasm for the prospects' projects. Remodelers report that many potential clients, who decided against a company, have said of other companies, "He [or she] didn't seem to really want my business." The successful remodeling salesperson will always clearly communicate a desire for the business and an appreciation for the chance to work on the proposed projects.

Determine Buying Style

Asking the prospects simple, interested questions is the first step in building rapport, but the questions do much more than just express interest. The way the prospects answer the questions, the topics they want to discuss, and the time they spend gives remodelers a great deal of information needed to determine the prospects' buying styles.

A buying or social style is the way that a particular person buys products and services. It is the way in which a person wants decision-making information presented, and it governs the specific types of information that the prospect believes are most important. Everybody buys goods and services for a different reason. Determining a prospect's buying style helps the remodeler decide on the best way to present the information about the company to improve the chance of closing the sale.

Once a person's buying style is recognized, the remodeling salesperson (a) shifts the presentation to give the most important information for that buying style first, (b) translates this information into benefits that will best influence the decision, and (c) delivers it in the format the prospect prefers.

If the remodeling salesperson can learn the buying style of the individual, the results could increase greatly because he or she will be better able to respond to the prospect's buying hot buttons or major concerns.

If remodelers ask the right questions, listen closely to the answers, and pay attention to the way a prospect answers, this process can become the most effective way to determine the buying style of a prospect. How the professional remodeling salesperson relates to these different buying styles makes a huge difference in his or her success. The key is to learn to listen closely. Someone once said that the best actor is a salesperson. This trait can come in wonderfully handy as the remodeling salesperson adjusts his or her presentation to fit the personality and buying style of the prospect.

The remodeling salesperson gathers information at the first call and picks up clues about the prospect's buying style. In most cases the remodeler will have a period of time to (a) assimilate the information, (b) translate it into features within the project that would provide the benefits the prospect wants, and (c) prepare a presentation that fits the buying style—all before the next meeting. So while buying styles are important to the success of the sale, the remodeler should not concentrate on this one aspect at the expense of other important information.

The remodeling salesperson determines how to present his or her solutions, the major benefits, and the important aspects of the project based on the type of buyer the client is.

Basically, knowing the prospects' buying styles helps the remodeler develop a product and presentation that closes the sale by relating the company's products and services to the specific needs of the client.

Defining buying styles is often instinctive to highly successful, professional salespeople. And even though they might not be aware of it, they probably unconsciously modify their presentations to fit the different personalities of their prospects. Buying style information is one more tool to help the remodeler make a more effective sales presentation.

Most psychologists agree that people are made up of a combination of the four major buying styles discussed in the paragraphs that follow.

Type A—These people want to be in charge and are concerned with facts and figures. They will ask questions and want straight answers. They will not sit through a bunch of fluff before they can get to the meat of the presentation. They maintain a businesslike relationship with the remodeler or remodeling salesperson, while they ask him or her to get to the bottom line. They want to know that the product will work effectively and efficiently to meet their needs. In dealing with these people, remodelers or remodeling salespeople should not waste time with small talk. These people make their expectations clear.

I compare this type of buyer to a powerful floor sander. In order to get it to go where you want it, you have to direct it gently and let it go.

—Mark Richardson
Vice President
Case Design\
    Remodeling, Inc.
Bethesda, Maryland

If the buyer were a Type A, the presentation would be a businesslike explanation that included the bottom-line results. The remodeler would point out how the proposal meets the needs stated at the previous meeting and show the prospect how the proposal for the project provides the results the prospect wants.

The remodeler would not waste this prospect's time with detailed descriptions of the esoteric aspects of the project. "I compare this type of buyer to a powerful floor sander," says Mark Richardson, vice president of Case Design\Remodeling, Inc., in Bethesda, Maryland. "In order to get it to go where you want it, you have to direct it gently and let it go."

Type B—Outgoing, friendly, and enthusiastic are characteristics of these buyers. They are fast-paced and want to have a trusting relationship with the people with whom they associate. They want the reasons why one company or solution is better, and they tend to make decisions quickly. These buyers are likely to pay more because they like the remodeler, but they can be impatient and want results quickly. These people are more interested in the big picture rather than details.

The Type B buyer would be excited about the big picture. After presenting the overall solution, the remodeler would give the prospect time to ooh and aah before rushing into the details of the project.

Type C—A relaxed and informal atmosphere sets the stage for these buyers. These people are much slower paced. They want to know about how their projects will affect their lives and improve their lifestyles. They want to have a relationship with a particular remodeler or salesperson. They will not make quick decisions, and they will be ready to deal with things other than just business. These buyers are more interested in feelings and emotional buying motives.

With a Type C buyer, the remodeler would spend more time translating features into the benefits of added comfort, style, and enjoyment. The presentation would talk about lifestyle enhancements instead of the practical, physical details.

Type D—These people are quite conservative. They weigh their information carefully and take their time about making decisions. They probably are not attracted to luxuries but lean more toward the practical. These people will want to justify their purchases with sensible reasoning and evidence that the investment will pay off in the future.

For example, if the remodeler or remodeling salesperson determines that the prospect is a Type D—the practical, no fad buyer—he or she probably would not close the sale if the proposal included an expensive jacuzzi or exotic materials. Knowing the prospect's buying style, the remodeler or remodeling salesperson would stress sturdy, attractive materials that will maintain their value for years to come throughout the presentation.

Observe Body Language

Another way to learn about a prospect is through body language. The experienced remodeling salesperson watches closely for non-verbal signals of approval or dislike. He or she also makes sure not to invade the personal space of the prospect. Everybody has a certain personal space that they do not want invaded. If the remodeler or salesperson insists on getting physically too close to the prospect, the prospect could become uncomfortable. A professional is aware of this possibility and stays well within the prospect's comfort zone.

Smiles, nods of agreement, and leaning forward are all signals that the prospect likes what the remodeling salesperson is saying or the questions that he or she is asking. The remodeling salesperson works to elicit these types of signals because he or she wants an enthusiastic response from the prospect. The remodeling salesperson needs to constantly monitor the situation to make sure that the prospect is not bored, indifferent, or upset.

If the prospect is sitting back, frowning, with arms crossed, the remodeler salesperson can assume the prospect is not happy with some part of the meeting. Many professional remodelers will stop at this point and ask, "I see that you're shaking your head. Is there something that you disagree with?" This question will bring the objection into the open and give the remodeler a chance to clarify a point and get the meeting back on track.

Is the prospect inattentive? Perhaps the remodeling salesperson is asking questions about details that do not interest the prospect. Is the prospect answering questions in monosyllables? Perhaps the remodeling salesperson is trying to wrest control away from a Type A prospect. Or is the remodeling salesperson talking too much and not allowing the buyer to talk about his or her dreams?

Keeping an eye on the nonverbal signals that are constantly being exhibited by the prospect could be the remodeler's or remodeling salesperson's secret weapon. These signals are especially important when the project includes two or more decision-makers. The salesperson must skillfully address each of the buying styles of the people involved.

Action Plan 3—Build Rapport

- When you go on a sales call, dress like the best-dressed person who might be there. Your appearance, presentation materials, and vehicle need to be neat and clean.
- Respect the prospect's property and treat it as if it were your own.
- Be forthright, open, and friendly when meeting the prospects. The tone set here will continue throughout the call and possibly for the entire job.
- Show a genuine interest in the prospect by spending the first portion of the meeting building rapport.
- Watch for clues to determine the prospect's buying style and modify the sales presentation to fit.
- Observe body language to obtain a multitude of clues toward the prospect's interest and attitude.

Chapter 4

Gather Information

Buying is an emotional process rather than a logical one. As sales expert Tom Hopkins says, "Logic is a gun without a trigger."[1] The trigger is emotion. Most people are buying a product or services to meet an emotional need. Whether the need is safety, comfort, or financial security, people will buy to satisfy this need. "It's up to the salesperson to involve the prospect on an emotional, gut level—to go beyond the logical decision making level," says Howard Goldstein, Director of Training, Sandler Sales Institute, Rockville, Maryland. "Identify their real reasons for doing business. Look for the why, not just the what."

It's up to the salesperson to involve the prospect on an emotional, gut level.

—Howard Goldstein
Director of Training
Sandler Sales Institute
Rockville, Maryland

This situation is especially true in remodeling. People do not buy new appliances and cabinets just for the sake of having new appliances and cabinets. They buy the benefits these products provide: enhancing the appearance of their homes or making food preparation easier. People do not add a major addition just for another room. They build an addition to give them the benefits of that room, (for example, the privacy and solitude in a master bedroom and bath), or they might add an elaborate deck to allow them to enjoy the garden that they labor over.

Selling Is Listening

Bring Needs to the Surface

Many remodeling prospects, however, are not aware of all of their emotional needs. The remodeler must help the prospects bring their needs to the forefront for two reasons. First, making the prospects conscious of all of their needs shows them that they must consider this potential purchase on many levels. Second, the more needs that the remodeling job can address, the better chance the remodeler has of closing the sale.

During the information gathering phase, the remodeling salesperson has several goals:

◆ Discover the needs and wants of the prospect.
◆ Determine the priorities of these needs and wants.
◆ To have the prospect confirm the priorities.

33

◆ Communicate that the remodeling salesperson is on the prospect's side and will work to give him or her a solution that meets these needs.

The remodeling salesperson must discover the true needs of the prospect in order to design the right solution to meet them. Sometimes a prospect can communicate one or two outstanding problems such as a need for more space for a household with three children or the need to upgrade and modernize an urban condominium. But possibly several other needs are right below the surface, unconsciously steering the decision-making process. The remodeler might discover that clutter is driving a prospect crazy. What the prospect really wants is less confusion in the home. The remodeler could answer this need with creative built-in storage in a smaller addition at a price the client can afford.

Many prospects will discuss their remodeling needs with several companies' representatives before deciding which company will actually get the work. Remodelers estimate that 90 percent of their prospective customers also talk to one or more other remodeling companies before making a final decision.

The remodeler who presents the most comprehensive solution that meets both the client's logical and emotional needs will be awarded the job. To develop such a solution the remodeler will wisely ferret out all of the prospect's motivations at the first interview. The key to discovering these motivations is to ask questions, listen, and observe.

Look for Physical Clues

Besides the actual verbal answers that a prospect may give to a remodeling salesperson, many other physical clues will give direction. "My first job on this call is to listen and look around," says Tim Wallace, president of T. W. Wallace Construction, Inc., Arlington, Virginia. "The clues I pick up from the environment can make a major difference in how I design and present the project."

How does the homeowner keep the home? Is it impeccably clean and formal or is it cluttered and casual? If the home is spotless, this prospect is quite likely to be much pickier than the casual homeowner. The fastidious housekeeper may want to know in great detail how the company controls dust and maintains cleanliness on the job.

Is the decor traditional, contemporary, or eclectic? Style and taste are extremely personal. If the home is furnished with wingback chairs and English chintz, the homeowners are not likely to buy a soaring, modernistic addition, no matter how interesting. On the other hand, if the home is filled with original paintings and sculpture, suggesting inexpensive products to save money may not be necessary. "I can tell within the first 5 minutes what the prospects standard of value is," says Jack Hertig, president of

Hertig Building and Remodeling, Inc., in Elkhart, Indiana. "What I see immediately tells me if they buy quality to last forever, or prefer to buy throw-away stuff. I look for the quality of detail."

Does the household include children? Taking a T-shirt or coloring book to the next meeting will show that the remodeler or remodeling salesperson cares and is thinking about the family. No parent will fail to notice. Are pets on the premises? A considerate remodeler or remodeling salesperson will detail how the company protects pets.

What type of car does the prospect drive? If a Mercedes is parked in the driveway, these prospects are probably interested in top-quality products and services and would be willing to pay more for it. If a Yugo is the family transportation, concentrating on giving value for the money usually would be the smart move. This time the remodeler might not want to get carried away with creative and expensive suggestions, even though they would be wonderful for this particular project. "Cars can fool you though," says Hertig. "Don't rely too much on the car."

What is the neighborhood like? Is the prospect's home the most expensive or the least expensive in the neighborhood? How much of an investment would overimprove the home for the area? The remodeler is the prospect's expert consultant, and the consultant is responsible for recommending the best way to invest the prospect's remodeling dollars.

Ask Questions About the Project

The prospects have been thinking about this project for weeks, if not months. Inevitably, they will want to jump right into talking about their projects, their major problems, and ideas for solutions. This enthusiasm provides a wonderful opportunity to ask plenty of questions about their dreams. A successful remodeling salesperson will take advantage of this opportunity to start the prospect talking. Many experts say a goal of successful salespeople is to get the prospect to talk 80 percent of the time and listen only 20 percent of the time.

Remodeling salespeople need to take note of more than the most obvious aspects of the project. Savvy remodelers read between the lines and ask the right questions to get below the surface. To prepare the prospect, the remodeling salesperson might say, "In order for me to help you create just the right change in your home, I'd like to ask you a few questions?"

Leading, open-ended questions may uncover information and unearth hidden needs that effect the final proposal.

Uncover Objections

In addition, in-depth questions help objections surface early in the sales process. Asking about previous remodeling experience will prompt the prospect to talk about previous problems they might have had such as the inconsiderate subcontractors or a hard-to-reach contractor. These questions give the remodeler the chance to deal with these objections early rather than at the end when they could derail the entire project.

Further Qualify the Prospect

The answers to these questions will also help further qualify the prospect. If a budget range was mentioned during the initial telephone call, probing questions can confirm that the prospect's concept of a realistic budget is, indeed, correct. By finding out what the prospect does for a living, the remodeling salesperson can pretty accurately discern if the project is within reach.

The budget range must be confirmed at this time. Otherwise, the remodeler could waste great amounts of time working on a proposal that will be out of the ballpark. Or in the other direction, the proposal could include many cost-saving features, when the prospect is looking for luxury.

In addition to uncovering needs, possible objections, and confirming budget range, nonthreatening questions will show that the remodeler is interested and will communicate that he or she is indeed working with the prospect to design the best value for the money.

The goal of the remodeling salesperson during this information-gathering phase is to get the customer talking, to find out what particular needs they would like to have fulfilled and what their priorities actually are. Open-ended, probing questions beginning with who, what, when, why, how, and where, require more than a one-word answer and provide the most information.

The remodeler asks, "What are some of the features that you'd like to see in your new addition," instead of "do you want a fireplace?" He or she might ask, "How do you prepare meals in your home," or "when does the kitchen area seem most congested?" These questions will encourage the prospect to open up and think through their needs clearly. The remodeling salesperson does not ask questions that can be answered in one or two words, such as, "Do you want two ovens or one?"

Other typical open-ended questions include those listed in Figure 4-1.

These questions can be customized for the specific type of project. The more complex the project, the more questions should be asked. Jeanie Morrissette, principal of Homestead Construction in Annandale, Virginia, says, "I think women are particularly good at asking detailed questions about the habits, likes and dislikes of the family. It's easier for a woman to ask personal questions such as if the prospect prefers showers to baths, or if they stand up or sit down when they put on their socks. But the answers can help you design a project that truly works for them."

By taking in as much information as possible, the remodeler

> ## Figure 4-1. Typical Open-Ended Questions
>
> ◆ If you had the freedom to build whatever type of addition you want, what would you choose?
> ◆ When did you move into your home?
> ◆ Why are you thinking about remodeling?
> ◆ How long have you been thinking about this project?
> ◆ How would you handle this problem if you don't remodel?
> ◆ What happened to cause you to pursue it now?
> ◆ What bothers you most about the home (building) you currently have?
> ◆ What do you like best about your home now?
> ◆ What difference are you looking for?
> ◆ What atmosphere do you want your home to have? Formal, casual, comfortable, clean?
> ◆ How long do you plan to live in your home?
> ◆ How often do you entertain?
> ◆ What will be the main use of the family room?
> ◆ How would you like your friends to describe your home?
> ◆ What are some of the details that you'd like to have in it?
> ◆ What style of home do you like in general?
> ◆ Who will be using your new addition most often?
> ◆ Who will be involved in the final decision?
> ◆ What would help you have a better-organized home?
> ◆ How important is the return on your investment?

can refer back to the prospect's answers when presenting the solution. At the next meeting the remodeler might say, "You mentioned that you still wanted to be able to see your children playing even after the addition was built. You can see that we've taken this into consideration when designing your addition and have built in several windows that give you a full view of the backyard."

Turn Information into Opportunity

The remodeling salesperson can turn each small piece of information he or she receives into an opportunity to present a solution that is unique and that cannot be copied or initiated by competing companies. This attention to detail will go a long way toward selling the remodeling company.

Answer the Needs of Two or More

If the remodeler is meeting with two or more prospects, all of whom have a say in the purchasing process, the remodeler should pay particular attention to the signals that pass between the parties. Commonly both people will be looking for a solution to one major problem or need. But each of the decision-makers also has certain needs that are not shared. Phil Branstetter, president of R. L. Rider Design and Construction, Inc., in Lansing, Michigan, says, "You have to be sure to give each person equal time. Even if one seems to be the decision-maker, ignoring the other person can be a major mistake."

If one person is concerned about cost and return on investment, but the other wants the best products possible, the remodeler can expect a conflict. Experienced salespeople will resolve this situation and actually make it work for them by proposing a project that meets the common need but has something extra for each. Products that are top-of-the-line but will last for years would satisfy both of the people in the preceding example. Each will hear the information that is most important to him or her.

Take Notes

The successful remodeler does not rely on memory. Each answer is written down on the spot. These answers will be referred to again and again. Plus, the homeowner notices that the remodeler takes his or her opinions seriously.

Practice, Practice, Practice

Successful remodeling salespeople readily become familiar enough with a list of these open-ended questions to ask them smoothly, comfortably, and naturally. If necessary, they practice these questions until they are second nature. Some remodelers, like Doug Off of Douglas Design in Tacoma, Washington, actually uses a survey form at the meeting. "This is an extensive, 15-page survey," says Off. "Sometimes we will send it to the prospects and ask them to begin filing it out before we get there. This [survey] is a great method for encouraging them to think about their projects ahead of time." Adding two or three new questions to each client presentation is an excellent way to increase the information that the remodeler obtains.

Confirm the Details

One common problem that remodeling salespeople run into is that they think they know what the homeowner wants but find out differently when they present the design solution and estimate. At this point, the remodeling company has already dedicated hours of valuable time to the project. Better to find any miscommunications at the first call, when they can be easily straightened out, rather than after developing an unacceptable proposal. If the salesperson returns with a solution that solves the wrong problems, rarely does the firm get a second chance.

Remodeling salespeople can avoid this disaster by verifying and confirming the most important pieces of information with the prospect before leaving the first call. Summarizing and paraphrasing the information back to the prospect will give him or her a chance to clarify specific issues and point the salesperson in the right direction.

Successful remodelers do not assume that they know what their prospects want. They restate the needs and priorities in the sales presentation. Each person has different experiences and a different idea of what he or she would like. The remodeler must make sure that everybody involved in each particular project has the same perception of that project. The professional salesperson regularly stops the questioning process with a review, "Let's summarize the information we've discussed so far," or "let's take a minute to review your priorities" are two simple ways to confirm. During this discussion the remodeler looks for definite agreement from the prospect. If it is not forthcoming, the remodeler goes back to the information-gathering stage until the prospect can confirm the details.

This portion of the sales process is probably the most important one in relationship selling. A popular maxim says that people are not sold, instead they buy. The better prepared the remodeler is to develop the right solution, the more easily prospects can buy their services.

The remodeler's knowledge of the prospects' needs will drive the success of any sales opportunity. Pertinent, open-ended questions, listening skills, and observation are the keys to this important advantage.

Action Plan 4—Gather Information

- Go beyond the prospect's obvious reasons for remodeling and discover the emotional reasons to help you to create the solution that will entice the prospect to buy.
- Ask in-depth questions during this interview phase to uncover objections and deal with them instead of waiting until later in the sales process when they might delay the sale.
- Confirm the budget range at the first meeting.
- Give each person at the meeting equal time. Avoid assuming that one or the other is the real decision-maker.
- Take extensive notes rather that relying on memory.
- Watch for physical clues such as furnishings, styles, and the prospect's manner of dressing. These clues can clarify the direction that the design should follow.
- After spending 80 percent of the meeting asking questions and gathering information, review the prospect's priorities with him or her to avoid miscommunications.

Chapter 5

Present Your Company

Once the remodeler has explored the problems with the prospect, he or she is ready to talk about the features of the remodeling company and why this company should be the prospect's first choice. During this opportunity to do the talking, the remodeler should let the enthusiasm ring out.

Naturally, the remodeler is proud of the company and is eager to talk about the features that make it special. But instead of just pointing out every company feature, he or she will focus the presentation to give the prospects specific information that responds to the concerns they had mentioned earlier. The remodeler concentrates on why these distinctive features are an advantage and what each means in benefits to the prospects.

Every remodeling salesperson should know exactly what benefits are delivered to the prospects because, after all, these benefits are really what interests the prospects. One helpful sentence that many remodelers and remodeling salespeople use to make this transition easier is "This *feature* offers this *advantage* which provides this *benefit* to you." For example, instead of just pointing out that the company employs its own crews and does not use subcontractors, the remodeling salesperson adds, "this arrangement means that we can control our quality of installation to a greater degree, which means you will receive the best job possible."

A remodeler who uses subcontractors might say, "All of our subcontractors have worked with us for 10 years or more. They know how particular we are about quality, and they meet our high standards. So you can be assured that only experienced workers will be assigned to your project."

Anyone can claim that his or her company is the best for the job, but the direct evidence is the proof. Today potential customers who are about to make a large purchase usually like to (a) gather a lot of information about the selling company and (b) be sure that the firm is qualified and experienced. This situation is particularly true of the remodeling industry. Because of some past unscrupulous contractors, remodelers today have to work harder to prove to their prospects that they are truthful, honest, and professional businesspeople. The more evidence and information that the remodeler offers, the more likely he or she is to make the case and establish this crucial credibility.

Professional salespeople know that sales tools can be invaluable in presenting this evidence about their companies. Information makes a much greater impact when it is presented both verbally and visually. Sales tools give the verbal message a concrete backup.

In addition, a prospective client is much more likely to believe hard, physical evidence than a verbal statement from a remodeling salesperson. In fact, many people are extremely skeptical of anything a salesperson says, but more easily believe information presented in other ways.

The presentation book sells the benefits of a remodeling company. This remodeling sales tool is a physical representation of the remodeling company. It contains the evidence of the company's qualifications and demonstrates the qualities that set this company apart. It once was known as a pitch book. However, with today's understanding and appreciation of the relationship sales process, remodelers do not pitch their services anymore. But they do need to present the materials that represent their companies.

Company in a Can

Because the book is the company in brief, the quality of the look and feel of the presentation book is unconsciously transferred to the remodeling company itself. This transference provides an excellent argument for investing in an outstanding display. If a remodeler wants to present an excellent, high-quality image, the presentation book should be created to support it (Figure 5-1).

Investing in a rich leather, three-ring binder or a neat, professional artist's portfolio could be one of the wiser investments a remodeler can make. As for any purchase, the high-quality material will look better for a longer period of time and is a much better value for the money. Mark Bartlett of River Crest Design/Build in Annapolis, Maryland, states, "We've invested over $1,000 in our presentation book. Since the book displays our company, it's important that it look top quality. Our philosophy is that if it isn't a great presentation book, don't bring it to the appointment."

Mark Goldsborough, president of Mitchell, Best, and Goldsborough, Rockville, Maryland, and his staff do not use traditional presentation books. Instead they have developed a beautiful full-color, 8½x11-inch, 20-page brochure that is used to present the company (Figure 5-2). "When we use the brochure, we can simply leave it with the prospects after we've walked them through it," says Goldsborough. "Everything about our company is explained right there."

Some remodeling companies, such as Plath and Company of

Figure 5-1. Presentation Book

MGD Design/Build Company, Silver Spring, Maryland, uses a well-designed presentation book that incorporates before-and-after photos as well as sample sketches.

Figure 5-2. Brochure Used in Lieu of Presentation Book

Source: Mitchell, Best and Goldsborough, Rockville, Maryland

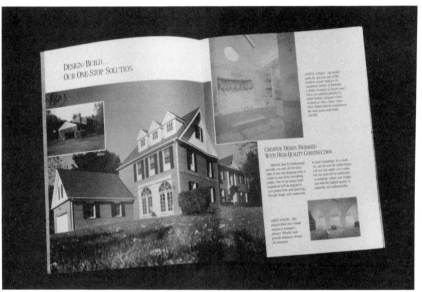

San Francisco, use a presentation folder to describe their companies. Like the brochure, it also becomes a leave-behind packet. (See Figure 5-3.)

Compare this look with a book that started out as a cheap binder from the local discount store and is now dirty and scratched. Would this send the right message to a prospect? The company presentation deserves time and effort, an adequate budget, and a thought-out plan to make it a workable tool.

Don't Miss a Trick

Presentation books should tell the company story and present information in a logical order. This arrangement helps the prospects to take in a lot of information without becoming confused. It also makes the presentation easier. After giving the same

Figure 5-3. Presentation Folder for Prospects

Plath and Company of San Francisco uses a three-panel, 9x12-inch folder with a stepped-down pocket to display easily replaceable, single pages that describe various projects the company has completed. The insides of the panels provide other information about the company. While some sheets focus on residential projects, others display commercial work. Thus the packet can easily be customized for a particular prospect.

presentation over and over, some remodeling salespeople get bored with it and begin skipping parts that they may think are marginally important. But this practice can be the undoing of an otherwise successful sales call. The salesperson can never be too sure which detail will appeal. And the prospect just might base a decision on the one detail that the salesperson left out.

However, if the remodeling salesperson is using a presentation book, important information is included on each page. Skipping over a page of benefits becomes harder to do if it is right in front of the prospect. The book forces the remodeler to go through the presentation consistently and to include all of the pertinent data that support his or her claims of excellence and know-how.

Tell the Same Story

Presentation books are particularly important for a company with more than one remodeling salesperson. After going on sales calls for many years, most remodelers develop a method of presenting their company with which they feel comfortable, and that method seems to work best for them. Their presentations also include supporting materials that have been collected over the years.

This practice works fine for the owner of the remodeling firm who also does the selling. If other salespeople are brought on board, they do not have the same experience as the owner nor the same important supporting materials. These salespeople could wing the presentation and could miss some important points. But each person who is presenting the company to the public should tell the same story. Each one does it in his or her own personal style, but the story should be consistent. By preparing a comprehensive presentation book for each remodeling salesperson, the remodeler can be reasonably certain that an accurate, complete story is being told in a way that best presents the information.

Of course, each salesperson needs a certain amount of leeway to create a book that reflects his or her work and personality. But this additional data should be in conjunction with the standard company information and should measure up to the graphic look of the rest of the book.

Enhance the Information

A comprehensive graphic look for the presentation book can turn the mundane into the excellent. Information that is beautifully arranged and attractively presented to the prospect is more interesting, entertaining, and easier to digest.

A computer with desktop publishing software helps to create materials that look professionally designed and typeset. While many companies do not have this option in-house, they can easily obtain it from such outside sources as a local printer or a freelance graphic designer. A high-quality card stock or other heavy paper (such as the mat papers used in framing) should be used in one basic color throughout. Adding a second or third mat in a complementary color will give the photos and other materials in the book a professional appearance.

All materials should be mounted in the same orientation, either horizontal or vertical. Few things are as annoying as constantly being forced to turn a presentation book back and forth to view the materials that it contains. This distraction could ruin the level of concentration that the remodeler has built. An artist's portfolio or oversized binder allows enough space for letters, awards, and photos to be placed in the same orientation.

Include the Crucial Ingredients

But what should go into a presentation book? When preparing a presentation book, the remodeler should consider the image that will be left with the prospect. Does the company want to be known for one particular type of job such as decks, kitchens, or additions? If so the presentation book should have a strong representation of this type of project.

If the remodeler wants to increase the number of additions the company does and to move out of the smaller jobs, the book should emphasize these jobs and play down the smaller projects. So the presentation book and the presentations done with it mirror the project goals of the company.

In addition, a presentation book allows the remodeler to educate the prospect about remodeling in general and the specific attributes of his or her company. The book should contain materials that support these benefits and promote them to the prospect.

Company Information

Some of the best presentation books begin with a statement of the company's philosophy. This brief paragraph or two discusses the goals of the company and its service to its customers. This statement points out that the remodeler is aware that customers are the most important part of the business. Prospects will appreciate this outlook and will respond to the respect it shows for them.

A brief history of the company would show how its strengths have developed over the years. Photos and biographies of the principles would follow. If a remodeler is willing to be represented in a photo as president of the firm, the prospect is more likely to believe that he or she will stand behind the company's work.

The Staff

Many companies include photos of their top people with brief biographies illustrating a wide range of expertise. These remodelers emphasize the staff's unique education or work experiences that add a special quality to the company. If personnel change, the remodeler can easily change the presentation book to reflect the current staff. Some companies with more than one employee use a group photo. However, making changes requires rescheduling a group photo shoot, which can be time-consuming. To many people, a staff indicates a company's stability and permanence.

The Office and/or Showroom

If a remodeler has an outside office, a photo of it should appear in the presentation book. This visible business location reassures the prospect that the company will be around in the coming years. After all, the company has invested in this office, which they would not have done if they were not intending to be in business to support their customers in the years to come.

The same philosophy applies to a company showroom. The company that has devoted funds to a showroom should include a photo.

Associations and Organizations

Respected, long-term companies often belong to a number of community and trade organizations. These memberships demonstrate a desire to support the community and stay on top of industry developments. This approach to business impresses many prospects. They are often pleased to see that the remodeling company is giving something back to the people who made them successful. The presentation book should document membership certificates or honors.

Many remodelers include trade references and list in their presentation books their suppliers, banks, insurance agents, and subcontractors complete with contact names. Again, this practice shows the prospect that the company is a responsible business.

Insurance and licensing documents are essential elements for a presentation book.

Third-Party Testimonials

Testimonials or third-party endorsements will take care of any cynicism about the facts that the remodeler presents. These testimonials can come in many formats, all of which should be included and used in the company presentation. One of the strongest testimonials is the acknowledgement of awards that the remodeling company has won. Showing off award-winning projects reinforces the company's image as a high-quality firm.

Other testimonials include copies of articles that have been written about the company or articles that quote a company owner or employee. These articles establish the quoted person as an expert resource for others. If publications editors and writers are calling the remodeler for information, chances are that the prospect will be impressed and will be inclined to trust the opinion of the remodeler even more.

But the best type of testimonial is happy letters from previous customers praising the company's performance. Nothing means as much to the prospect as a satisfied client who thought enough of the services of the remodeler to take the time to write a letter. The prospect knows that a customer would not have written a letter if he or she were at all unhappy with the service, so these letters pack a whollop.

Since most prospects do not want to take the time to read each and every letter, many remodelers highlight one or two sentences that capture the essence of the previous customer's message. This practice lets the prospect quickly spot the message that the remodeler wants to convey.

Another form of the satisfied-customer letter is a completed company evaluation. Many companies send evaluation forms to their customers after their projects are completed. Favorable evaluations confirm the remodeler's claims of efficiency or professional business practices. Including a slightly negative letter or evaluation and documenting the follow-up to correct the situation also impresses prospects.

Before-and-After Photos

For most prospects the photos are the icing on the cake. Viewing the large, colorful, professional photographs of the company's completed projects is the fun part of the presentation for the client. No matter how well a remodeler can shoot a photo, he or she is not likely to equal the quality a professional photographer can produce. A less-than-excellent photo can be a major detriment to a remodeler's image. A budget to shoot several projects professionally should be built into each year's marketing budget. "Using less than professional quality photographs doesn't do you any favors," says Tim Wallace, T. W. Wallace Construction, Inc. in Arlington, Virginia. "Good, clean professional photos gives the prospect a clear idea of your work. Plus, if they're comfortable with what's shown in the photos, they're less likely to feel the need to do a lot of research in checking out the company."

These top-notch photos should be used as large as possible in the presentation book. The company's actual work is going to be the final convincing factor for the prospect. The remodeler should be proud of the company's work, display it in a way that shows that pride, and not skimp on the photographs of finished projects. Before-and-after photos add realism and a wonderful sense of how greatly the remodeling improved the house or building. Each photo needs a caption to (a) identify the project, (b) give a few details about the problem, (c) and tell how the remodeler helped to develop the solution to the problem. "We include the investment costs for each project along with the photo," says Guy Semmes. "We want them [prospects] to know exactly how much remodeling really costs. This [cost information] might be a rude awakening for them, but we want them to feel the pain right up front. This is a great way to find out if they're comfortable with the investment."

Teach Prospects the Process

All of this information helps show the prospective client that the company is reliable, reputable, and does its work well. In addition, a presentation book can also help to explain the exact process of a remodeling project. Clients who understand the different steps involved are less likely to demand unreasonable changes or to question the remodeler once the job is underway. Therefore, many remodelers choose to walk the prospect through the documents that are used throughout the process.

Beginning with the initial contract, the remodeler will include samples of completed forms so that the client can see an actual contract, change order, estimate, preconstruction conference checklist, and a punchlist. These forms show the huge amount of detail that is involved and also demonstrate the company's thoroughness. The document and the remodeler should explain why the forms are used and why they are important to the prospect. This explanation is especially useful for change orders and punchlists because these stages often cause conflict.

If the remodeling company also offers design, a sample floor plan, and perspective sketch let the homeowner know what he or she can expect to see from the company in terms of design illustrations. The more the prospect knows what to expect, the less chance that he or she will be disappointed. The majority of prospects have never been involved in a remodeling project previously and have no knowledge of the many steps that are involved.

The presentation book is only one tool that can be used to enhance the information given to the prospect. Some remodelers use other sales aids such as manufacturers brochures or product samples. "Since we do a lot of kitchens, I know that kitchen cabinets will probably be necessary," says Jack Hertig, Jack Hertig Building & Remodeling, Inc., in Elkhart, Indiana. "So cabinet samples are an essential part of my presentation. I want them to be able to feel the product and become involved right away. The samples can also be used to begin talking about the levels of quality that are available." The photography in manufacturer's brochures can help prospects visualize different styles and help the remodeler begin to get a sense of their taste levels.

A great deal of information can help to convince the prospect that this company fits the job. However, each person will have particular areas of interest that the remodeling salesperson has noted. The successful remodeler, while mentioning or touching upon all of the crucial information, will spend the majority of the time tying in specific details with the needs expressed earlier in the meeting.

If the client had mentioned reading a story about an unreputable contractor leaving town after collecting a downpayment, the remodeler would be sure to stress his or her company's years in the business and its prominent office location. If a client expresses dismay at the length of time the neighbor's project took to reach completion, the remodeling salesperson could explain the production flowchart and detailed scheduling process. On the other hand, if a prospect clearly is not interested in reading the many different categories in an estimate, the remodeler does not spend much time on it. Again, the remodeler's notes from the information-gathering phase of the sales call provide clues to the information to stress.

Just as an automobile salesperson would not begin a lengthy discussion of engine-power advantages to a prospective customer who obviously is not interested, neither should a remodeler spend an inordinate amount of time on technicalities in which a prospect is not interested—no matter how important this information is. The remodeling salesperson should remember the buying style of the prospect and fit the company presentation to that style and that interest level. The salesperson does not have to tell the prospects everything he or she knows. He or she focuses on just what the prospect needs and wants to know.

Considering the amount of information that can be included in a presentation, a remodeler could spend hours discussing each and every detail. However, few clients would agree to spend this much time. Normally, a company presentation is completed within 15 to 20 minutes. The brevity of the presentation makes even more paramount the need to get to the priority information that will drive the prospect's decision.

Take the Next Step

Ask for Commitment

Before the remodeling salesperson leaves the first meeting with the prospect, he or she should be sure that the information that (a) has been gathered is correct and (b) that both parties have a common understanding of the next step. This task requires the salesperson to ask for a minor commitment. No remodeling salesperson should leave the first call without receiving at least a small commitment from the prospect to ensure a strong chance of closing the sale.

The final discussion at this first meeting clarifies what will happen when the remodeling salesperson and the prospects meet again. Commonly, the salesperson hopes to leave the second meeting with a commitment, either a design contract if the company offers design build or a signed construction contract. The salesperson should make sure that the prospects know what he or she is planning to deliver and what the next step will be if the remodeler does meet their needs.

A remodeler might say, "Our next step is to use the information that you've given us today to develop an idea to use as a starting point for your project." At the next visit we will present a rough floor plan and perspective sketch, and we also will have an estimate prepared to show you how your investment might be allocated. In all likelihood, we will make plenty of changes, but this information will be a starting point for further discussion.

"At our next meeting, we'll be asking you to make a decision. If we're able to present an idea that you agree is a good starting point, we'll ask you to move into the design phase which I've described earlier. Does this sound good to you?"

Remain Silent

At this point, the remodeling salesperson remains silent until the prospect replies. Many salespeople make the mistake of jumping in with another statement or question and get nervous because of the silence. In order to really discover if the sales process has been successful, they have to wait for the prospect's response. To become disciplined at this, some remodelers begin to count to 10. Often, the prospect will begin to speak well before the count of 10 is finished.

However, if the prospect hesitates or offers yet another objection, the remodeler must once again back up to the information-gathering or the presentation stages before going any further. Obviously, if the prospect will not agree to this general condition, the remodeler missed something in an earlier phase of the sales process and an unaddressed concern lingers.

By telling the prospects what the salesperson expects from them, the salesperson prepares them to make a decision. If they agree that he or she understood their needs, they know that they will be expected to make a decision. No misunderstandings will occur at the next step.

Set Up the Next Appointment

The professional salesperson sets up the date and time for the second appointment while he or she is at the first meeting. The prospect knows that the salesperson will be returning in a reasonable amount of time, and this act of discipline by the salesperson means less chance that the meeting will go into indefinite hold or be delayed beyond a reasonable time.

Keep Prospects Involved

Homework

To maintain the prospect's enthusiasm until the remodeler gets back with solutions, many remodelers give the prospect a small piece of homework to accomplish before the next meeting. This homework might be a trip to the bath showroom to review the varieties of sinks and vanities that are available. Or it could be to drive by two or three of the remodelers' completed projects to look at a particular design or style. This homework helps the prospects get involved in the process, so they are not just observers. When prospects are participating in the entire process, their anticipation and excitement stays at a higher level.

Leave Behind Packets

Both parties have given and received a great deal of information has been given and received by both parties. A leave-behind packet full of information reminds the prospect of the specific company information and helps him or her to set one company apart from another. Included in this leave-behind packet might be a list of customer references, a copy of a company brochure, and reprints of articles about the company. While the packet is not intended to be nearly as complete as the presentation book, it will reinforce the pertinent points that were discussed during the meeting.

Follow-Up After the First Meeting

The next step, done immediately after the first appointment, is a follow-up, thank-you letter that confirms the time and place of the second meeting. This follow-up letter is a simple, considerate touch that lets the prospect know that the remodeler is excited about the project and appreciates the opportunity to talk about it. This gesture sets the company apart from its not-so-organized or professional competitors. This follow-up letter should not be complicated or time consuming, and it should be part of the remodelers sales system and used after every initial appointment. A standard letter can be easily prepared, customized, and sent out in minutes. Whether the letter is in the computer and ready to go with a few minor changes or has to be typed each time, using one perfected letter as the standard will speed up the process greatly.

This letter also provides an opportunity to reconfirm the major needs of the prospect by mentioning them briefly in the standard letter. A paragraph would begin as follows:

When designing your new addition, we will pay particular attention to the areas we had discussed including—

◆ Producing a creative window treatment in the southern exposure to expand upon the open feeling
◆ Providing privacy from the close-by next door neighbors
◆ Protecting and not disturbing the large oak tree in the backyard.

"We have a letter in our computer that has five or six areas that can be specific to the job," says Goldsborough. "This follow-up makes a wonderful impression on the prospective buyer." By customizing a small portion of the letter and restating a few major points, the prospect will know that the remodeling salesperson did listen and will be more likely to feel well-served.

Develop a Presentation Book

Start with an attractive binder or portfolio. Check it every few months for wear and tear. Include the following items—

◆ A short company history or philosophy—no more than three paragraphs—emphasizing the company's strengths
◆ A copy of each required license in your geographic area (Explain its need to the consumer.)
◆ Certificate of insurance showing required liability and Workers' Compensation insurance (Explain the importance of this contractor's insurance to the homeowner.)
◆ Membership certificate for a remodeling association and other professional and business affiliations
◆ Community association membership certificates (Belonging to the Chamber of Commerce, the Better Business Bureau, and the like should all be documented.)
◆ Before-and-after photos (They can provide an opportunity to discuss budget and style considerations.)
◆ Awards won by the company
◆ Articles about the company or the remodeler
◆ Programs listing the remodeler as a speaker

While all of these items would be included, a remodeler would emphasize only those pieces of information in which the prospect has expressed interest.

Action Plan 5—Present Your Company

- Plan to spend no more than 20 percent of the total appointment time on presenting the remodeling company to the prospect.
- Use sales tools, such as presentation books, copies of letters, product samples and brochures, to increase the prospect's retention and add credibility to the salesperson's claims.
- Invest in an attractive presentation book as a physical representation of the company.
- Make the presentation book comprehensive because you can never assume that you know what information will make a difference to the prospect.
- Use the information gathered earlier to match the remodeling company's benefits and features to the concerns and interests of the prospects.
- Before you leave the first appointment explain what will be expected of each party during the next step. Tell the prospect that he or she be asked to make a decision at the next meeting.
- Send a customized follow-up letter after the first meeting as a professional touch that shows the prospect that the salesperson was listening and that, once again, confirms the prospect's priorities.

Chapter 6

Present Solutions

Finally, time for the second meeting arrives and provides the salesperson a chance to display the creative and expert solutions that the company has developed for the prospect's problems.

Usually several days to a week pass before the remodeler's second appointment with the prospect. If the remodeler has an office, often he or she prefers to meet the prospect there, on the company's turf. This meeting provides an opportunity to show off the facility, to confirm that the remodeling company is, well-established and stable, and to introduce the prospect to other members of the staff. "By having the second meeting in our offices, we control the meeting to a much greater degree," says Ted Brown, Traditional Concepts, Lake Bluff, Illinois. "Besides giving the prospects a feeling of confidence by meeting in a real office environment, it's much easier to keep the prospect's attention. Since there are no distractions, such as kids running about or the telephone ringing, an effective meeting takes about 40 percent less time than it does when it's held in the home."

Of course, some remodelers always go back to the prospect's location to present their ideas and talk about possible solutions. This practice is fine, especially if the remodeler does not have an office that will reinforce the image that he or she has worked so hard to create.

This meeting is essentially a working session to present ideas for solutions that can serve as the trigger for brainstorming until the remodeler develops a design that pleases the prospect.

Review and Confirm

Before showing the prospect the actual ideas, the remodeling salesperson starts by reviewing the overall strategy of the remodeling project—the problems that had to be solved. A well-prepared presentation might include an outline prepared specifically for this client. This outline would list the major needs that were agreed upon at the first meeting. The prospects would each receive the outline to use as the remodeler or remodeling salesperson reconfirms the information guiding the solutions. Jerry McDaniel, president of McDaniel Remodeling Company, Inc., in Tucker, Georgia says, "We try to be very specific at this stage. We create a nicely bound, personalized presentation booklet that has our logo on the front. I always take at least three copies so that everyone there [receives one and] feels important."

After reestablishing the relationship with a few moments of small talk, the "remodeling salesperson would say enthusiastically, "I think that we've developed some ideas that you're really going to like. But before I show you the actual sketches, let's go over our last discussion. You had several specific problems that you wanted solved by remodeling your home. He or she would refer to the outline and reiterate the last meeting, reminding them of the detailed discussion and begin the meeting by asking the prospect to agree and in effect sign off on the information at the beginning of the meeting.

A great deal of time seems to be spent in reconfirming the prospect's needs and wants as the remodeler goes through the various stages of the sales process. A lot of time is spent on this issue because the remodeler must understand the prospect's needs completely. And the prospect must agree with the remodeler's assessment. This agreement must occur if the remodeler is going to close the sale.

After obtaining agreement, the remodeling salesperson needs to demonstrate the company's expertise. Many salespersons do this with a detailed estimate and preferably a sketch of how the remodeling project might look.

Sketches—Visual Selling Tools

While some remodelers do not offer sketches of their design ideas, increasingly they present their solutions visually to support a verbal walk-through of the estimate. Just as the visual selling tools help create and reinforce the image of the remodeling company, the selling sketches can help close the sale. "I'm a firm believer in the use of design visuals," says John Sylvestre, president of Sylvestre Construction, Inc. "People would have a very difficult time making sense out of a design without sketches. The visuals make a huge difference in the effectiveness of the sales call."

Most prospects cannot visualize the finished product the way the remodeler can. In most cases, even a sketched floor plan is too abstract. Perspectives and elevations, no matter how rough, will better communicate the product to the prospect, and in turn, they will generate excitement and desire. A sketch of the new addition or kitchen is what will capture the imagination of the prospect. He or she can picture the furniture in the room, see a cookout on the new deck or imagine children playing there.

The selling sketches do not have to be elaborate or artist's quality, but they should give the prospect a good idea of how the changes will affect the property. When a prospect can imagine living or working in the new space, the remodeling salesperson is halfway to the sale.

Jeff Clark, vice-president of Metropolitan Design and Building in St. Louis, Missouri, says, "Visuals are all important to the sale. Without them no one can understand what you're trying to communicate. Plus, they're essential to getting over the hurdle of price." Metropolitan Design and Building provides . . . [its] clients with sketches [Figure 6-1] and, on occasion, models of the project that is under consideration. "Three dimensional models are an excellent way to show wonderful details about the way the project will be built," says Clark. "Plus, the clients love them."

Sylvestre Construction has begun using a computer program that allows their designers to see the project in three dimensions (Figure 6-2). "We can look at the project from below or [into it from above] . . . ." says Sylvestre. "Then we can rotate it to see the project from any angle. Once we have the right view, we print it out and take it to our client." Sylvestre's eventual goal is to use this computer program in conjunction with a client meeting to generate an immediate response.

Compare the situation outlined above with this scenario using just a simple estimate. The remodeling salesperson returns for the second meeting armed with nothing more than the breakdown of the costs. Even if he or she walks the prospect through the estimate and mentions all of the items that add value, the estimate will not have the impact of a selling sketch. The estimate provides nothing to get the prospect excited and counterbalance the anxiety produced by looking at the high investment involved.

Remodelers have many ways to produce a sketch without investing a great deal of money. If the company is not a design build firm, but works with an architect for the design portion of the project, perhaps the remodeler could work out an arrangement with the architect to provide a simple sketch at the beginning of the sales process. Some remodeling salespersons do simple designs themselves using a magnified "before" photo as the template for the changes. Others use a freehand sketch. At this stage, the sketch just demonstrates creativity and expertise, and it serves as a communications tool for the prospect.

Tim Wallace, president of T. W. Wallace Construction, Inc., Arlington, Virginia sketches the possible design solutions while discussing them with the prospect. "I'll just sit and do a line drawing right on the spot," says Wallace. "I want to be sure that we're on the same track and a drawing is an excellent way to describe my ideas. Since we're discussing the project at the same time that I'm drawing, the prospect gets involved and becomes emotionally invested in the project."

Of course, the amount of time that a remodeler will want to spend greatly depends on the size of the job. Even companies that regularly prepare sketches for large projects do not invest the time or money if the project is small in scale. Limited options may make a sketch unnecessary for small jobs.

Design build firms offer top-quality design as part of their entire package, so these types of companies must demonstrate their design capabilities when they present their solutions to their prospects. A design build remodeler uses the design phase as an opportunity to ask for a monetary commitment ranging from a low of $200 for preliminary sketches to 5 percent of the construction estimate for elaborate working drawings. While remodelers

Figure 6-1. Drawings of a Proposed Addition

Metropolitan Design and Building, Inc., provides its prospects with a floor plan and perspectives of interiors and exteriors of proposed additions. Prospects find that visualizing the end result is much easier when design sketches are used.

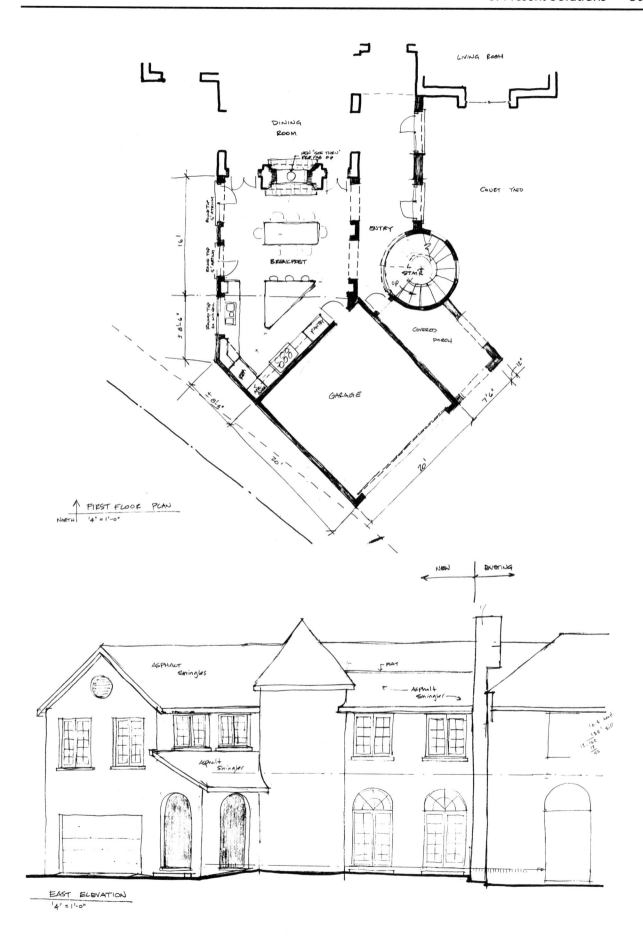

LIVING ROOM

DINING
ROOM

COURT YARD

ENTRY

BREAKFAST

STAIR
UP

COVERED
PORCH

PANTRY

GARAGE

20'

20'

7'6"

12"

↑ FIRST FLOOR PLAN

NORTH   ¼" = 1'-0"

NEW   EXISTING

ASPHALT SHINGLES

PLAT

ASPHALT SHINGLES

ASPHALT SHINGLES

EAST ELEVATION
¼" = 1'-0"

Figure 6-2. House Model

John Sylvestre, president of John Sylvestre Construction, Inc., Minneapolis, Minnesota, uses models to demonstrate visually how the company intends to build a new project. "A model is an expensive investment, says Sylvestre, "but most people have difficulty visualizing a blueprint in three dimensions. A model can allow the clients to see the addition from all directions."

usually charge for this phase of the process, a prospect does not have to commit to the entire project at one time. He or she can still back out if proceeding is not comfortable. The prospect might believe that committing to a smaller investment is less risky, and the remodeler often finds asking for it easier. Joe Leonard, sales director for Hopkins and Porter Construction, Inc., Potomac, Maryland, says, "By committing to even a small investment, they are showing their commitment to me and my company. Any form of commitment means that I'm that much closer to the sale."

As the remodeling salesperson presents the design, he or she should talk about benefits more than features. He or she can use the transition statement that was mentioned earlier, "This feature offers this advantage, which provides this benefit to you." For example, the remodeler says, "We'll use 2x6s for studs instead of the usual 2x4s. This size gives you more stability and lets us install thicker insulation. This extra insulation means that your energy bills will be smaller. I know that you are particularly concerned about utility costs."

The remodeler focuses on the benefit to the customer and how a particular feature will make the project even better. Not only does this show the company's expertise, but it also tells the prospect that the remodeler has listened to his or her concerns and cares about them.

Later in the presentation, the remodeler might comment, "This portion of the addition will be cantilevered out about 3 feet. This design feature means that we won't have to disturb the roots of that oak tree that you love so much. We didn't want to take any chances with that." If the remodeler did not point out how the design offers these benefits, the presentation would have much less impact on the customer.

Throughout the presentation of the solution, the remodeling salesperson should be asking for agreement from the prospect. "We took advantage of this southern exposure by adding glass transoms above the french doors to the patio. We know that you wanted the kitchen to be as light and bright as possible. How do you like this design?"

Each agreement the remodeling salesperson can prompt makes achieving an agreement on the entire project easier. While he or she certainly would not ask for agreement on every small detail, the prospect must concur on the major items. This process can be woven into the presentation whether selling sketches are used or not. The successful remodeler also tries to demonstrate creativity and initiative by incorporating one or two special unrequested design elements into each project. "We always build in one or two special details," says Jeanie Morrissette, principal in Homestead Construction, Inc., in Annandale, Virginia. "If we're doing a kitchen, we might include a built-in soap dispenser. It shows our expertise and initiative. Even though it's just a small item, it's something that is used every day. And every time they use it they'll be thinking of our company."

Design Options

Because of the difficulty of perfectly meshing the initial design idea with the vision of the prospect many remodelers offer two or three quite different ideas for the prospect to choose from. The prospects may really like one element from sketch A and one from sketch B. By showing several options, the remodeler or remodeling salesperson can show the creativity and originality of the company. Plus, several options gives the prospect choices and increases the chances for closing the sale. Again with large projects such as a complex two-story addition, the project is unlikely to close even on the second call. "While we might only show the prospect one sketch at this point, we stress that it isn't the only option—just a point of departure," says Ted Brown.

For a simpler job such as a basement remodeling with no structural work, if the remodeler plans to get a commitment at this second meeting, he or she might prefer to offer alternatives. If only one option is presented, and it does not appeal to the prospect, the company could be out of the running. By showing several options, chances are that the prospect will find enough to like that one outstanding design can be gleaned from those presented. "We [believe that a prospect choosing from options is] . . . like a child picking out what to wear," says Mark Bartlett. "With too many options, [the child will] . . . get confused. But if you told him what to wear, he probably wouldn't like it. So the best solution is to give [a prospect] . . . two or three workable options to choose from."

Some prospects have a definite idea of how their projects should be designed. Often, their ideas are not the best solution. Remodelers have to walk a narrow line between offending the prospects and presenting the solutions that would better solve the problems. "We get around this by walking them through our process," says Alex Dean, president of The Alexander Group, in Silver Spring, Maryland. "The second meeting is called a working session. We'll show the prospect's . . . idea in a sketch. Then we'll talk about how we played around with the idea and came up with some other thoughts that might improve it. They'll usually agree with us and end up with our original design."

Presenting solutions is also a time to sell up or show the prospects how they can receive much more for a small increase in their budgets. Most people are concerned with costs and believe that they can only spend a certain amount. But, as in selling cars, homes, or clothes, if prospects see something that they just cannot live without, they can often find the additional money needed to have it. Successful remodelers often take advantage of this tendency by creating two or three optional designs for the homeowner to consider. As with a car, the options would be the basic, the midrange, and the luxury model. All of the options fit the basic needs, but the customer receives more amenities as he or she moves up the investment ladder. The successful remodeling salesperson never assumes that the basic model is all that the prospect wants.

Action Plan 6—Present the Solutions

- Spend a few moments to reestablish the rapport that was created previously.
- As the first step at the second meeting, review the information gathered at the previous meeting and make sure that the prospects still agree.
- Use visual sketches to help the prospect visualize the finished product. Once the prospect can imagine the project, he or she is more likely to want to move ahead.
- Point out the many details in the sketches that set the proposal apart from the competition.
- Limit the number of design options to help you guide the prospect to the solution that best fits his or her vision. Too many options can be confusing.
- Use sketches to sell up or demonstrate to the prospect what could be done with a slightly increased budget.

Chapter 7

Overcome Objections

In relationship selling, the salesperson would address possible objections throughout the call. In an ideal world, by the time he or she is ready to ask for the business, no additional objections should exist. However, this situation rarely, if ever, occurs. Inevitably, objections will surface at the many opportunities to do so. Therefore, remodeling salespeople need to know the common objections and be ready to counter them at any time during the sales presentation.

Objections as Stepping Stones

An objection is one of the most useful tools in the sales process because it gives the remodeler additional information that allows him or her to move closer to the sale. A hidden objection is a roadblock to a sale. An objection brought out into the open where it can be addressed becomes a stepping stone to a successful sale. Viewed this way, an objection is less likely to be perceived as a stall or as a poor reflection upon the salesperson or the company.

Many remodeling salespeople avoid digging for objections because they are afraid to hear them. They think that if they can avoid talking about problems the prospect might not bring up any of them and allow the salesperson to sail right through the close with nary a hitch. This belief is potentially destructive. The remodeler needs to uncover any hidden obstacles to the sale, and the only way to make sure that they are all addressed and withdrawn is to dig for them.

The beauty of relationship selling is that the remodeler uncovers and handles objections throughout the presentation. During the information-gathering stage, the remodeler finds out about many worries and addresses them in the presentation stage. If done thoroughly, this process takes care of many possible objections. Almost inevitably, however, the remodeling salesperson has to go back to one or two concerns that were not answered to the prospect's satisfaction.

If the remodeler does not uncover these early in the process, the objections will rear their ugly heads again—and just when that possibility is least desired. One useful analogy is for the remodeler to think of objections as a number of open doors in a room. Each time a possible objection is answered, a door is closed. When all the doors are closed and the prospect is within the room, the remodeler has a successful sale. If a door is left open, the prospect can just walk through it and out of sight. In other words, if all of the objections are not addressed during the early stages of the meeting, those remaining will come up when the remodelers ask for the financial commitment. If they are not addressed, the remodeling salesperson will lose the sale. Whether the commitment is for a small project which should be made at the first meeting, or the design portion of a design build contract, the prospect will stall and search for additional reasons why he or she should not make an immediate decision.

Even though many issues are dealt with throughout the call, the remodeling salesperson's goal is to learn about and address every objection that might still be in the prospect's mind. Only if the prospect feels calm, soothed, and anxiety free will he or she feel comfortable in moving forward.

Commitment Questions

If the prospect has been asking commitment type questions such as—

◆ How soon could we have the project finished?
◆ When can we go to see some of your other projects?
◆ When will you have the design options back to us?

the remodeler could be quite certain that the prospect is ready to commit. After all, if the prospects are not interested in the company, would they care how soon the project could be started? Probably not. These sorts of questions are a definite signal that the prospect is ready to sign a contract. A successful remodeler trains him or herself to listen for these positive signs of a successful sale.

Trial Closes

However, receiving such a clear signal is not as common as any remodeling salesperson would like. So the next best thing is a trial close. The difference between a trial close and an actual close is that a trial close asks only for the prospects opinion while the close asks for a definite decision.

Unless the remodeler is certain that the prospect is ready to sign on the dotted line and answer yes to a closing question, most of them believe that a trial close, asking only for an opinion, is less threatening and easier to do. Because the remodeler is not actually asking for an order, if the prospect is not comfortable making a decision yet, the remodeler can gracefully retreat to a less-threatening position saving face for him or herself and the prospect.

Even when asked for their input, some people do not feel comfortable stating their objections, but for his or her own benefit the remodeling salesperson must make sure that the presentation was effective and that no unknown objections will pop up to ruin the possible sale. Uncovering any hidden objections early allows the salesperson to bring them into the open, discuss them, and eventually neutralize them. A professional remodeler does not want to find him or herself dealing with objections after assuming that the job was in hand.

A trial close incorporates open-ended questions that will uncover any objections that may have remained hidden. The answers to the trial-close questions give the remodeling salesperson a good idea of how well he or she has performed the information-gathering phase of the meeting.

Asking the prospect, "How do you feel about the company?" or "Is this what you had in mind?" invites the prospect to ask more questions or to bring up an issue on which he or she is unclear. Questions from the prospect are welcome because they allow the remodeler to clarify the proposed project and continue to sell the benefits of the company. Other open-ended trial close questions include—

◆ What do you think about the way we structure the design phase of the project?
◆ What are your thoughts on the different steps in the process?
◆ What do you think of the additions you saw in the book?
◆ What were some of the design details that you liked the most?
◆ Is this what you had in mind?

The remodeler listens to how they answer as well as to what they say. If the prospect's answer is positive ("It sounds great!"), he or she is on the right track. If the answer is uninterested or noncommittal ("It's okay.") additional probing questions will reveal why the prospect is not enthusiastic. The noncommittal answer is just a cover for real objections, which the remodeler or remodeling salesperson must discover.

In the typical remodeling sales process, the remodeler does not ask for the final commitment at the first appointment. He or she takes the opportunity to go back to the office and work out possible solutions to the prospect's problem before asking him or her to sign a construction contract.

When addressing objections, the remodeler shows empathy toward the prospect and understands his or her feelings. The remodeling salesperson shows respect for the prospect and the prospects right to these concerns. If the remodeler views objections as challenges that must be crushed, he or she is in trouble.

Feel-Felt-Found

One of the best ways to show this empathy and respect and to lead right into the discussion of the specific objection is the feel-felt-found method. This method lets the remodeler or remodeling salesperson make sure that they truly do understand the specific objections and neutralize them in a soft, nonabrasive manner. First, the remodeler would acknowledge that the concern exists by restating it. "Let me make sure that I understand. You're not sure that you should make this investment in this house, right?" The next step is to show the prospect that he or she has every right to have this concern and to feel the way he or she does.

"I understand how you feel. You're right to look at your return on investment. It is wise to look at how this remodeling project would impact your home if you should ever choose to sell."

Then the professional remodeler tells the prospect that deciding to go ahead is a wise decision. "Many of our customers have felt that way until they saw the average sales figures for their neighborhoods. When they've looked at the numbers, many of them have found that an investment in remodeling was an excellent idea." Validating this claim usually eliminates this objection.

"In this area, the median home price is $180,000. Your home (which you said you bought for $130,000 about 2 years ago) is one of the few in the neighborhood without an addition. If we created additional living space but limited your investment to the range of $40,000 and $60,000, which is the budget we'd discussed, you will be well within the acceptable sales price for the neighborhood. So you can see that investing in this project will give you the living space you need now, and will also be a good investment if you should decide to sell in the future." The salesperson will support this claim with real estate facts or other research.

Another example: "You think that the price is too high for the addition, right? I understand how you feel. This addition is not a small investment. Getting the quality that you want in it is going to cost a bit more. Other customers that we've had over the years have felt that way too. But when they found out about our exacting standards, and the expertise of our personnel, they knew that they were going to get the best addition for the price."

Another way to make sure that the remodeler or remodeling salesperson understands the specific objection, is to restate the objection and ask for clarification from the prospect. "You're concerned that the new windows won't look good with the rest of the house, is that right? What exactly has you concerned?" This technique will encourage the prospect to begin talking, which will uncover the information needed to confront the real objection.

Ted Brown, president of Traditional Concepts in Lake Bluff, Illinois, reviews a script of the common objectives and the best reply before every sales meeting (Figure 7-1). "This review helps me be confident that I'll know how to react when an objection comes up in the meeting."

Figure 7-1. Common Objections and Successful Responses

Prospect: I'd like to think about it.
Remodeler: What exactly are you going to think about? *or* Earlier, you mentioned that you've been thinking about remodeling your home for several months. What are you still troubled about?"

Prospect: We'd like to talk to a few other companies before we make a decision.
Remodeler: It's always a good idea to find a company that you feel comfortable with and confident that they will do a good job. I hope you feel that way about our company.

Prospect: Oh, we do. We think you'd probably do a good job.
Remodeler: Why do you believe that you should talk to other companies? Don't you agree that our company will deliver a good value for the money?

Prospect: Your price is too high.
Remodeler: It is a large investment and you're right to be concerned about the value that you'll receive. Let's look again at what you'll be getting for your money.

Prospect: We'd like to talk about it, and we'll get back to you.
Remodeler: Is there something particular that you'd like to talk about?

Prospect: No, we're just not ready to make a decision right now.
Remodeler: I obviously haven't given you the information that you need to make you comfortable in making a decision. Let's review the proposal again to see where I may have missed answering your needs.

Prospect: It's just not what we were looking for.
Remodeler: Well, let's brainstorm and talk about how we can make this project just the way you imagined it!

Action Plan 7—Overcome Objections

- Ask the right questions so that any objections will be brought up and dealt with early in the sales call.
- Be prepared for objections to surface again when you ask for the financial commitment.
- Listen for closing questions from the prospects that mean they are ready to buy.
- Use trial close questions first because they are less threatening for the prospect and easier for many remodelers to use. These questions ask for opinion instead of commitment.
- When the time to close arrives, confirm that the solution meets the prospect's needs. That accomplished, you are ready to move into the close of the sale.

Chapter 8

Ask for the Sale

With all of the qualification that has been going on during the entire sales process, the remodeler should feel quite confident in the prospect's desire and ability to move forward. He or she should be ready to take the next natural step and ask for the business. After all, this step is part of the job. But the close of the sale will not be successful if the remodeler did not do a good job during the earlier portions of the meeting.

While additional meetings might fine tune estimates or designs, the remodeling salesperson should be reasonably certain of the likelihood of success and be able to get a commitment at the second meeting. Especially with small jobs, he or she should be able to close the sale at this point. Large jobs may require a greater investment of time and a few additional meetings before the contract is signed, but the prospect will be committed to the project with that remodeler. Design build companies in particular should be able to close at least the design portion of the project at this point.

Types of Closes

The following paragraphs describe a variety of techniques that successful salespeople use to ask for the business and close the sale.

Minor-Major Close

This closing technique asks the prospect to make a series of minor either-or decisions before asking for the major commitment. These minor decisions could be on—

◆ cladding material ("Would you like vinyl siding or cedar?")
◆ shingles ("Black or grey?")
◆ other options ("Would you like the bay or the casement window in the kitchen?")

The remodeler simply begins to ask these questions and writes down the answers. At the same time, he or she completes the contract. With each decision, the prospect is committing him or herself further. If the prospect does not object and makes these decisions, he or she usually is ready to buy.

Assumptive Close

With this method, the remodeling salesperson assumes that the prospect is buying and simply asks for the information that will let him or her move ahead. In an assumptive close, the remodeler would ask closing questions, for example, "Is Tuesday a good day for the preproduction meeting?" or "We can start construction a week from Thursday. Does that sound good to you?" The remodeler expresses no doubt that his or her company has been chosen to do the project.

"We always assume that we have a sale," says Mark Bartlett, vice-president of River Crest Design Build in Annapolis, Maryland. "I have that attitude from the very first call. When it's time to close, it's very natural to presume that . . . [the prospect] will go ahead."

Simply Ask Close

The remodeling salesperson simply asks the prospect to take the next action toward beginning the project in this popular close. He or she asks, "May I have your okay on this contract in order to put your project on the schedule?" and holds out the contract with the pen for a signature. Another question might be, "May I have a downpayment today so that we can schedule you immediately to ensure that we'll finish well before the holidays?" With this last statement, the salesperson is giving the prospect an added incentive to take action now.

Think-It-Over Close

More than any other objection, the one that stumps remodelers is, "We don't want to make a decision today. We want to think it over. Give us a call back next week." When hearing this response, many remodeling salespersons think that the prospect is serious and will truly take the time to evaluate the proposal. Because the remodeler feels confident, he or she will leave the plans and agree to call back the next week. When they do call back, the prospect has not taken the time to think through his or her doubts and still is not ready to decide whether to go ahead with the project.

The remodeler should try to avoid this situation. It simply means that the prospect still has concerns that the remodeling salesperson has not adequately addressed. He or she must dig to find the real objection. The key is to deal with it right on the spot. Once a salesperson leaves the prospect without a decision, the chances of closing the sale drop drastically. However, if the remodeler has prepared the prospect to be ready to make a decision at this point, he or she can avoid this dilemma.

Some prospect's will still offer this stalling tactic, and this next closing technique can help overcome the think-it-over objection effectively.

When a prospect offers this objection the remodeler could respond with understanding:

Remodeler: Well obviously you're interested or you wouldn't take the time to think it over. You have to make sure that you're making the right decision about this important investment. But I want to be sure that I understand where you stand. Exactly what do you need to think about? Is it the integrity of my company?
Prospect: Oh, no. Your company seems very good.

Remodeler: Is it the quality of our work?
Prospect: No, I can see that you do good work.

Remodeler: Is it the floor plan?
Prospect: No, we like your designs.

Each time the prospective client says no, he or she is confirming the positive aspects of the project.

The best way to use this close is to begin with questions concerning aspects of the job that probably would not cause the prospect a problem, such as company integrity or the salesperson personally and work down to the nitty-gritty items that might be the cause of the prospect's concern. If all of the other answers to the question, "Is it . . . ?" are negative, the time has come to ask about money. The remodeler ends the series of questions with "Is it the money you will be investing?" (For more positive results, remodeling salespeople would use the concept of investment instead of cost.) Chances are that the prospect will answer something like this, "Yes, we're just not sure that we want to spend that much, and we'd like to think about it some more." The remodeler at least knows that the price is the real issue. After asking, "Besides the investment, is anything else bothering you about the project," this question confirms that only one obstruction stands in the way of the sale, and the remodeling salesperson can concentrate on handling that issue.

It-Costs-Too-Much Close

When the prospect says, "It just cost more than we planned," the remodeler needs to backtrack. Obviously he or she may have made a mistake in the information-gathering stage. The remodeler should avoid designing to an unknown budget because this issue can be dealt with much earlier in the sales process. However, some prospects must be sold (and even resold) on the value that they will receive for their dollars.

One response could be, "You're right that this isn't a small amount. And I can see that you aren't sure that you're going to receive value for your money. Let's go over what your money is going to buy for you."

The remodeler goes back over the proposal and points out every feature and its specific benefits. As in earlier parts of the sales process, the remodeler will ask for agreement all along the way. Usually, a specific objection will surface at some point. "These Low-E windows are quite expensive. Why do we have to have those?" The remodeler can respond with the information that will show the prospect exactly how he or she will benefit from the windows or some other product or service. Once they have gone through the estimate again, another close is appropriate.

If the homeowner insists that he or she simply cannot afford the products recommended, the remodeler may suggest alternative products so long as he or she tells the homeowner that the alternative will not offer the same benefits but could be an adequate replacement if costs must be cut. Of course, the remodeler should not offer to lessen the quality until he or she has thoroughly explained the numerous benefits of the higher quality product. Some remodelers may allow sweat equity on a job, but only on activities that come after construction (such as painting), so the homeowner's work does not inhibit the smooth flow of production.

Don't Count on the First Time

As a rule, a remodeling salesperson would not attempt a close until he or she is quite certain that the prospect is ready to buy. However, sometimes waiting is difficult. If the salesperson finds that an attempt to close has annoyed or disturbed the prospect, the best thing to do is to apologize for putting pressure on the prospect and back up to the trial close stage. The closing process is a series of steps forward and then backward until the salesperson has provided all of the necessary information and the prospect is ready to sign.

The remodeler may have to ask for the order several times before achieving a signed contract. Tom Hopkins, author of *How to Master the Art of Selling,*® states that even the best salespeople attempt to close up to five times before succeeding.[1]

Prospective clients are trained to be wary and protect themselves and their families by thoroughly researching large investments. They want to feel confident that they are making the right choice. Prospective customers need to be convinced. Many times, they need a slight push to make the commitment. The closing is intended to do just that—to give the remodeling salesperson the opportunity to properly answer any questions or concerns that might be remaining in the mind of the prospect. The purpose of a professional, practiced close is not to trick someone into buying something they do not want, but to give them the little push to go ahead with something they do want or need.

The key to using closes successfully is practice. Each response should be practiced so many times that it is natural and sounds like ordinary conversation rather than a canned response. Many professionals begin by writing down their top five objections and actually creating three scripted responses for each. They practice these responses out loud until they can respond naturally and without hesitation. "After all, you don't tend to get the same objections over and over," says Mark Goldsborough, president of Mitchell, Best, and Goldsborough, Rockville, Maryland. "The really difficult objections each come up only once or twice a year. That's why we have to continue to practice the entire array of responses so that we're always ready."

If the remodeler carries a small notebook containing all of the responses to the various objections, it provides an opportunity to review the responses for 5 to 10 minutes each day to ensure that he or she knows the responses by heart. Closing effectively is traditionally one of the weakest parts of a sales call. However, if a remodeling salesperson can learn several well-thought-out closing statements, he or she will find sales increasing dramatically.

Thermometer Close

Howard Goldstein, director of training, Sandler Sales Institute, Rockville, Maryland, encourages salespeople to use the following scenario to bring the sale to a successful conclusion:

> After you've covered perhaps three-fourths of your presentation of how your service will eliminate the prospect's pain, you can ask, "On a scale of 0 to 10, 0 meaning we just don't have a fit, and 10 meaning that you're ready to sign the contract and schedule a starting date, where are you on the scale?"
>
> You should hear at least a 6 or higher from your prospect in answer to your question. Once you get the answer, ask the prospect what he or she needs to get to a 10. Your job is not to accept a "5" or a "I want to think it over." Your prospect will volunteer his or her own objections when you ask this question. After you deal with the objections, you'll ask again, "Where are you now on the scale of 0 to 10? Once you get him to a 10, ask, "What would you like to do now?" He or she will remember what you told him earlier and will probably answer something like "Well, I'm supposed to sign something now, right?" Your job at this point is not to sell, but to let the prospect buy.

Action Plan 8—Ask for the Sale

- Become familiar with several techniques to bring a sale to its conclusion even though closing the sale can be a natural extension of the entire process.
- Avoid stalling tactics so you can receive an answer to the closing question. Even if it is a no, any answer is better than being strung along because you can deal with the objections. If you are stalled, you may lose the sale.
- Practice alternative closing questions so that you can ask them naturally.
- After you ask a closing question, remain silent until the prospect speaks even if you have to count to 10 to do so. Closing usually takes more than one attempt (often as many as two to seven). Use trial closes—seeking agreement on something minor—to help move the prospect closer to signing.

Chapter 9

Follow-Up After Signing the Contract

Once the contract is signed, the remodeler often is ready to move onto the next sale and the next high. However, prompt and continuing follow-up of the latest one ensures that the sale remains secure. After any large purchase, buyers normally experience a period of buyer's remorse and doubt the wisdom of their decisions.

The federal government acknowledges this buyer's remorse with two laws designed to protect the homeowner. The first, the Right of Cancellation, gives the consumer the right to cancel within 3 business days of the transaction date if (a) the remodeler personally solicits the sale and (b) the contract is made in the consumer's home or a location other than the remodeler's place of business. The second is the Right of Rescission which gives homeowners the right to cancel or rescind within 3 business days of the transaction if a security interest is taken in a consumer's principal dwelling and if the contract is considered to be financed (jobs with more than four payments). In other words, if the homeowner defaulted on payment of the completed contract, the house could be sold to pay the remodeler.

Some remodeling salespeople do not have a system in place to guard against buyer's remorse, which can be strong enough to scare the client into canceling the project.

Wise remodelers know that this feeling is natural and plan a follow-up with the client within a day or two of the contract signing. Even a simple telephone call passing along information about a product or particular question can be enough to bring back the prospect's enthusiastic emotions and reinforce the decision.

"Mrs. Jones, this is Dick Smith from Smith Remodeling," the salesperson might say. "I just wanted you to know that the sink you wanted will be delivered in plenty of time for a Thanksgiving completion. So you don't have to worry about not meeting that important schedule."

"That's great news," says Mrs. Jones. "Thank you so much for letting me know."

This telephone call let Mrs. Jones know that her project was going to proceed on schedule, but it did a great deal more than that. The call also assured Mrs. Jones that the remodeler was thinking of her and her project. She would not be lost in the shuffle. This confirms her decision to move ahead and also her choice of remodeler.

Until time for the next meeting, the remodeler should find a reason to stay in touch with the prospect on a regular basis—at least once a week. Even if the call is just a progress report, the prospect will be appreciative of the thoughtfulness. This attention adds to the professional image of the remodeling company and the remodeling salesperson.

The Salesperson's Responsibility

Before Construction

In some remodeling companies, the salesperson's responsibilities are limited once the contract is signed. One responsibility that the salesperson usually maintains is the preparation of the production or job file. In order for the production person to pick up the ball quickly, he or she must have information prepared by the salesperson that clearly spells out the details of the job. This information might include—

◆ two copies of the signed contract
◆ two sets of the signed plans
◆ the check for the signing draw or a receipt for it
◆ financing papers
◆ copies of all orders for materials
◆ a copy of the building permit if this is the salesperson's responsibility
◆ a key to the building
◆ special concerns such as pets, children, security, workhours, owner's quirks, and the like.

"Let's face it," says Phil Branstetter, president of R. L. Rider Design and Construction, Inc., Lansing, Michigan, "the best salespeople don't care about the details. They are aggressive, and somewhat money-hungry. Their goal is to get to the answer yes. That's how they hit their high. Everything else is a waste of time."

Because the transfer from sales to production is one of the most common places for problems to appear, a crucial step for the remodeler is to create a well-thought-out system that makes sure every item and detail is accounted for.

Alan Peyton of Oak Park Design, Inc., Oak Park, Illinois, realizes the importance of not missing even one piece of information. "We were finding that the same questions kept cropping up—

things like how far away from the doorway should the cabinets be hung, and where was the light switch to go. It was frustrating to have to keep calling the office. And it didn't do a thing for our customer's confidence level. So we incorporated these things into a very detailed system that answers every conceivable question for the production department. This [system] saves both the salesperson and the production department a great deal of time and money by getting it right the first time."

Besides gathering this material, the salesperson is usually required to participate in the preconstruction conference. He or she is the link between the customer and the production person or department—the one person with the best overall concept of what is about to happen. The customers have developed a rapport with the salesperson, and they must not feel abandoned by their main contact. So at this meeting the remodeler introduces the other members of the team and makes clear to the customers that the responsibility is now in the hands of their production contact. This preconstruction conference has several goals:

◆ Pass responsibility to the production person or department.
◆ Clarify exactly what is going to be constructed and what is included in the project.
◆ Explain how the production person or department works and how the customer can best work with that part of the team.

During Construction

During the course of the job, some companies require the salesperson to pick up payments, and others require regular meetings with the homeowner. "Each of our salespeople must schedule a weekly meeting with the homeowner," says Mark Goldsborough, president of Mitchell, Best, and Goldsborough, a design build firm in Rockville, Maryland. "I want to be sure that the job is moving according to plan and that the customer is happy."

Other companies ask that their salespeople relinquish control and contact at that point and leave the rest up to the production crew. "Production is handled completely by the lead carpenter," says Phil Branstetter of R. L. Rider Design and Construction, Inc., Lansing, Michigan. "The salesperson sometimes goes back to visit the job out of curiosity, but he really shouldn't waste his time. After all, the customers are really in love with the lead carpenter by that point. They don't care about the salesperson anymore. But they are living with the carpenter."

Change orders commonly are processed and estimated by the salesperson, who may also be responsible for presenting them to the client for approval.

"After the punchlist is finished, our salespeople will accompany the customer on a final inspection, just to make sure that they are completely satisfied," says Branstetter.

After the Job is Complete

Gift

Immediately after the completion of the project, the customer is usually at a high point in the remodeling cycle. A thoughtful, thanks-for-the-business gift can go along way toward extending the favorable feelings the customer has about the remodeling company. The salesperson should choose something that will have a long shelf life and will be noticed for a long period of time. Well-chosen gifts include a magazine subscription, a pen-and-ink drawing of the customer's remodeled home, or a brass planter with a long-living plant. This gift shows the customer that the company appreciated the business, and it also serves as a tool for referral leads. Neighbors, friends, and family may notice the gift, inquire about it and prompt a wonderful referral statement from the customer. A gift after the job is an easy way to cement the relationship that was begun at the first call.

Evaluations

The remodeling contractor needs to monitor the company's performance regularly. A customer evaluation form is a perfect way to solicit comments on the good and the bad attributes of the company. The evaluation form should be simple and easy to complete. For best results, the remodeler should send out the form within a month of the completion of the project and include a stamped, self-addressed envelope to make the process extremely convenient for the client. The salesperson can encourage a response by telling the clients in advance to expect it and why it is important to the company. If they know it is coming, they are more likely to take the time to complete it.

Incorporating a numeric rating system in the form makes the evaluation easy to complete and provides the company with a way to scientifically analyze the information. This system allows the homeowner to review the numbers to see exactly where improvements can be made. If efforts are made to improve a particular aspect of service, the remodeler ought to see an improvement in the numbers. (See Figure 9-1.)

Some remodeling companies will also send evaluations to customers who did not go forward with their projects. These evaluations allow the salesperson to see if the customers had any specific complaints, or if they chose another company, what the competition had to offer that his or her company did not. (See Figure 9-2.)

Telephone surveys can be done in either instance. The impromptu comments that a customer or prospect makes over the telephone can be quite revealing. Successful remodelers incorporate yearly telephone surveys of 5 to 10 customers and lost prospects into their ongoing monitoring systems.

The process of today's selling style is meant to create a long-

Figure 9-1. Client's Evaluation of Company

Company Name and Address

Name _____ (Please print)

(As you circle your ratings, please remember that a rating of 5 is excellent and a 1 is poor.)

1. How happy are you with the project design?   1 2 3 4 5

2. Was our salesperson courteous, helpful, and knowledgeable?   1 2 3 4 5

3. What was your main reason for choosing our company? _____

   _____

4. Was our production manager courteous, helpful, and knowledgeable? 1 2 3 4 5

5. Was our production manager responsive to your questions and
   concerns throughout the project?   1 2 3 4 5

6. Was our office staff friendly and efficient?   1 2 3 4 5

7. Were the people working on your job courteous, helpful, and neat? 1 2 3 4 5

8. Were the workers on your job well supervised?   1 2 3 4 5

9. Were our subcontractors professional and quality conscious? 1 2 3 4 5

10. What did you like best about working with us? _____

    _____

11. How was our overall performance?   1 2 3 4 5

12. Comments? _____

    _____

    _____

13. May we use you as a reference?   ☐ Yes   ☐ No

Please use the reverse side of this page for any additional comments. If you have rated us poorly on any section, we would appreciate any specific comments you might give us to help us improve our performance in that area. Thank you.

Source: Remodeling Consulting Services, Silver Spring, Maryland.

Figure 9-2. Lost Prospect's Evaluation of Company

Thank you for the opportunity to speak to you about your remodeling project. We want to deliver the best service and highest quality product available. If you would take a moment to answer the questions listed below and tell us why you did not choose our company, you would greatly help our efforts to improve our service. Thank you. We appreciate your assistance.

1. Have you awarded your remodeling contract to another remodeling company?
    ☐ Yes   ☐ No   If no, please move to Question 4.
    (Optional) Name of remodeling company who was awarded job. _____

2. Was your decision based on any of the following? If so, please rank them for importance.
    (1 for most important, etc.)
    ___ Timeliness of response
    ___ Salesperson's ability to accurately assess needs
    ___ Company's ability to present creative solutions
    ___ Professionalism of presentation
    ___ Personal rapport with salesperson
    ___ Previous relationship with company
    ___ Product offerings
    ___ Company's reputation
    ___ Price—If price was a factor, was the estimate from our company higher by—
        ☐ 0–5%   ☐ 5–10%   ☐ 10–15%   ☐ More than 15%
    ___ Other_____

    _____

3. How many times did you meet with the other company representatives? _____

4. If you did not proceed, why not? _____

5. Please rate our company representative on the following: (1 = poor, 10 = excellent)

Ability to listen	1	2	3	4	5	6	7	8	9	10
Professional appearance	1	2	3	4	5	6	7	8	9	10
Ability to understand your needs	1	2	3	4	5	6	7	8	9	10
Technical expertise	1	2	3	4	5	6	7	8	9	10
Creativity of solutions	1	2	3	4	5	6	7	8	9	10
Follow-up	1	2	3	4	5	6	7	8	9	10

6. Please tell us the main reason you did not choose our company._____

    _____

7. Other comments or questions. _____

    _____

    _____

Source: Reprinted with permission from Remodeling Consulting Services.

term relationship between the remodeling company and the client. However, some remodeling companies do not take advantage of the hard work that went into the previous stages of the sales cycle by doing an adequate job of following up after the sale. The remodelers who reap repeat business are the ones that realize that selling never ends.

Why Did the Company Lose the Job?

The remodeler needs to know why his or her company did not close a particular sale. The information behind the prospect's decision to choose another company or to put the project on hold can help the remodeler improve and to close more sales in the long run. A remodeler would send this survey form to prospects who did not award his or her company the job (Figure 9-2).

The survey should be short—no more than 2 pages—and appear quick and easy to complete. Again, including a stamped, self-addressed envelope encourages a response.

Action Plan 9—Follow-up After Signing the Contract

- Develop a system to avoid hitting buyer's remorse.
- Make a telephone call within the first 2 days to help the prospect feel comfortable and confident.
- Compile a comprehensive job file that includes all pertinent information to give to the production department.
- Use preconstruction walk-throughs and conferences as tools to transfer the responsibility for the project over to production and avoid miscommunication with the customer.
- Follow company procedures for moving to the next sale while maintaining ongoing contact with the customer.
- Follow-up after the job to extend the customers feelings of good will toward the remodeler and to help generate referral leads for the future.
- Continually monitor customers and lost jobs to obtain essential information for company improvement.

Chapter 10

Manage the Sales Function

Often a remodeler will find that he or she is working 60, 70, or even 80 hours a week struggling to keep up with all of the tasks that need to be done to keep the company in business. When this situation occurs, the remodeler needs to think about splitting up the duties, with the owner taking half and hiring another person to take the other half. Most commonly, remodeling company owners have come up through the craftsman ranks. As their companies grew, they needed more time for the sales functions while still acting as production supervisor and sometimes even working on the jobs.

Once a remodeler decides that he or she cannot do it all, the most logical move is to separate the production functions from those of the sales, marketing, and administration functions. Once these functions are divided, the owner of a remodeling company must take a hard, realistic look at what he or she does best, and how those attributes can best be used to meet the goals of the company.

John Mathis, a specialist in human resource development and president of Keyline Company, Inc., in Exton, Pennsylvania, comments, "The owner must look at his or her primary strengths and how they fit with the overall outcome of their business goals. That's where they should put their emphasis and hire someone to carry the other load."

If the remodeler is an excellent technician, with an innate knowledge of construction, he or she might find that hiring a salesperson will be the greatest help to the business. The key is to have the owner of the business focus on what he or she does best and hire someone else to help with the other aspects of the business.

While the common belief states that no one can sell the business as well as the owner, Mathis believes that, with the proper backup materials to add credibility, a well-trained salesperson can also do an exceptional job. "Salespeople are professional communicators," says Mathis. "They are in the business of representing a

> *The key is to have the owner focus on what he or she does best and hire someone else to help with the other areas.*
>
> —John Mathis
> President
> Keyline Company, Inc.
> Exton, Pennsylvania

company and, once trained about the specifics the company offers, should be able to bring in a healthy amount of business for the owner. The company can help with written materials, presentation materials, and even videos that help explain the company's position on quality and service."

"Profile the Job"

Once the remodeler decides to hire a salesperson the first step is to compile all of the requirements of the position in a comprehensive, written job description. Mathis calls this profiling the job. "Each owner has a different perception of . . . [his or her] company and how it fits into the community. He or she will have a totally unique view of what is needed in the company's salesperson. Writing down the specific requirements will ensure that the owner begins by looking for a person that will be able and willing to accomplish what is needed."

These specific goals might include a salesperson who will do the following:

◆ Actively solicit new business from the community.
◆ Represent the company by becoming actively involved in community organizations such as the Chamber of Commerce and the Rotary Club.
◆ Be dedicated to learning the specific features and benefits of the variety of products the company uses in its jobs.
◆ Accurately estimate jobs and sell them at an established average percent markup.
◆ Display an enthusiastic, optimistic attitude

The key to success in hiring a salesperson is for the remodeler to get specific. Only by carefully determining what the company needs will the owner be able to hire a person to fulfill those needs (Figure 10-1).

Remodelers must look at hiring as a priority task that uses a system that has been well thought out. The remodeler might consider this a bureaucratic nuisance, but a blueprint for the job will assist the remodeler in hiring someone with the needed skills and the right experience.

However, hiring the wrong person can have a detrimental affect on the company's bottom line. The costs would include salary, lost sales opportunities, loss of morale for the other employees, lost training time, and perhaps a deterioration of the company's reputation in the community. A remodeler should not be reactive and hire too quickly when another employee quits or is terminated.

Qualifications

Before soliciting applicants, the remodeler must list the qualifications required for the job including education, experience, and skills. To be legal, the qualifications must be job related and specific, specific enough to draw someone qualified to do the job, but

---

Figure 10-1. Topics to Include in Job Description

- Title
- Objectives of the job
- Dress code
- Hours
- Times and lengths of sales meetings
- Continuing education expectations
- Commission policy
- Direct supervisor
- Car allowance
- Specific responsibilities and duties
- Qualifications
- Relationships with others, both internal and external

---

not so specific that no one can qualify. They also should not be skewed toward a particular anticipated applicant so that only that person could comply. For some skills a remodeler might want to list the skill and a preferred form of that skill. For instance, a remodeler might want the salesperson to be computer literate so that he or she can easily use the firm's computerized estimating, billing, and lead-tracking systems. The ad could state that candidates need computer skills, with knowledge of a specific software preferred.

Solicit Applicants

Once the job profile or description is created, the remodeler needs to begin soliciting for applicants. If the remodeler is forward thinking, he or she has been keeping a file of possible candidates for upcoming positions. However, a remodeler who is searching for the first additional salesperson may not have developed such a file. He or she will have to use alternative methods for soliciting applicants. Ads in trade publications and local association newsletters can reach a qualified audience.

"Newspaper ads are still the best way to attract qualified candidates," says Mathis. "While the owner might get referrals, the chance that they will be good candidates is poor."

In preparing ads to solicit applicants for a salesperson's position, remodelers must be careful to comply with the laws regarding such matters. He or she should review the ad carefully to be sure it avoids potential discrimination references to the applicant's race, creed, color, national origin, sex, marital or family status, age, arrest record, or disability. For example, to be legal the ad should specify a salesperson rather than a salesman or saleswoman. Ads and interview questions should be carefully reviewed by an attorney or someone familiar with federal, state, and local laws pertaining to discrimination.

After taking applications, the remodeler can screen them according to who fits the basic job requirements, such as sales experience or knowledge of the construction industry. Once the applicants are screened, the select few are invited to an interview.

Interview Applicants

John Mathis describes his process, "When you run an ad for an employee, the law says that you must accept applications from everyone who replies. However, typically a large percentage of the applicants do not meet the basic requirements stated in the ad. [The wise remodeler would] . . . qualify the prospects before spending an inordinate amount of time in interviews.

"When prospective employees call in response to the ad, tell them that you are accepting applications and invite them to come in to fill out an application and a 15-question interview form. The results of these applications will tell you who meets your basic requirements and will narrow the field down to top candidates who are then invited in for an in-depth interview." To comply with the law, the remodeler must use the same process to screen each applicant. Legally the questions on the interview form must be the same for each applicant, and the questions must be free of any bias or discrimination based on the applicant's race, creed, color, national origin, sex, marital or family status, age, arrest record, or disability.

The carefully crafted job profile is the blueprint for the interview process. This description helps the remodeler prepare to listen for the information that will tell him or her that the candidate is a good match. The main interviews should last between 45 minutes and 90 minutes in order to get beyond the surface information.

Each applicant should be asked the same list of open-ended questions that have been carefully screened to eliminate potential bias or discrimination based on the applicant's race, creed, color, national origin, sex, marital or family status, age, arrest record, or disability. The remodeler should listen to the applicant's attitude as well as the direct answer. He or she should ask each candidate to describe previous positions and to provide lots of examples from the past such as:

◆ What was the most difficult sales call for you?
◆ What was your most important victory?
◆ What did you learn at your last job?
◆ Describe the best job possible.
◆ Describe the worst job possible.
◆ Describe the best boss.
◆ Describe the worst boss.
◆ What mistakes would you avoid doing again?
◆ How do you prepare for a sales call?

Personality Profiles

Many companies are now using comprehensive aptitude testing or personality profiles to dig deeper than the surface information that can be gathered by a traditional interview. These profiles look at such factors as the person's drive to succeed, what motivates them, how do they compare to other successful people in their field, will they be able to ask for the order, and how to best supervise and motivate them. These profiles can also measure the candidate's mental abilities, career interests, personality, learning ability, and energy level.

However, decisions cannot be based solely on the results of these profiles. They are simply a supplement to the traditional hiring methods. Hiring judgments must be based on the qualifications of the prospective employee.

Phil Branstetter, president of R. L. Rider Design and Construction, Lansing, Michigan, swears by personality profiles " . . . a personality profile is simply another tool that will help me hire the best person possible for my firm. If they don't possess the basic personality traits that are necessary for a successful salesperson, I don't want to hire them. For the small investment necessary, I wouldn't attempt to hire without it."

These profiles compare the candidate with the job description that the remodeler developed rather than comparing one candidate with another. By choosing the person who best matches the job description, the remodeler will probably spend less time on basic training. He or she will be able to move the new employee quickly into the more sophisticated aspects of the job. While the remodeler should not consider these profiles a panacea, they can supplement or confirm information that the remodeler has already gathered. Personality profiles are best used to differentiate the top two or three candidates that have already shown that they could fit the needs of the remodeling company.

Many different forms of personality profiles are available, but all profiles may not be legal to use in hiring. When choosing a format, the remodeler should do some research to determine if the profile instrument has been legally accepted and how long it has been in use. Checking with an attorney and the local Equal Employment Opportunity Office will help the remodeler avoid possible problems.

With or without a personality profile, the remodeler should look for openness in the candidate's style of communication. Since selling is 90 percent human relation skills, the prospective salesperson must be able to communicate clearly and persuasively. The remodeler should also attempt to determine the candidate's ability to follow rules and procedures. "Selling is made up of a number of rules," says Mathis. "Even a person who doesn't possess all of the necessary attributes can be successful if [he or she] . . . can follow the rules of successful sales.

That's why it's so important that the salesperson be able to follow the correct procedures."

Salespeople from Another Industry

Remodelers should also keep an open mind toward people who apply from outside the industry. The sales rules are the same from industry to industry. Basically, only the technical information changes. In the majority of cases, that information can be learned. Mathis says, "Sales skills are . . . transferable from one job to another. Again, it is the communication skills that make the difference in a salesperson who is hugely successful and one who is marginal." However, because of the technical nature of remodeling, not every salesperson can make the transition. For instance, salespeople who have difficulty seeing things on paper in three dimensions would have difficulty selling remodeling, and some cannot cope with the terminology.

Explain Expectations of the Job

Before hiring, the remodeler must find out if the candidate is willing to meet the expectations that the remodeler has for him or her. Saying, "I want you to get involved in the community," is not enough. This statement could mean many things to many people. Better to say, "I expect you to join the Chamber of Commerce and the Rotary Club, attend their monthly meetings, and join a committee. This activity will promote the visibility of our company." Such a statement could not easily be misinterpreted by either party. Every person is working from a different frame of reference. So what seems perfectly clear to the remodeler could mean something completely different to the salesperson. These expectations should be written in detail and agreed upon before offering any candidate a position.

The remodeler should also take the time to think about how each candidate will fit with any other employees and other members of the current team such as the production personnel, subcontractors, and others. Does he or she have the same work ethic? Will his or her selling skills and interpersonal skills mesh with the others? Hiring someone who will not easily fit into the team will be a mistake.

Check References

Even though the remodeler has spent a great deal of time interviewing and talking to a candidate, no person should be hired into a company before all of his or her references have been checked thoroughly. Discovering any problems at this point is better than after a person has been hired. Some recruiters recommend going beyond the previous bosses and acquaintances that the candidate provides by asking the references for references and calling them too.

Each application for employment should include a signed release to legally allow the remodeler to check the applicant's references.

After Hiring an Employee

Set Goals

Mathis recommends using the reverse income forecasting technique to set goals for the sales department. Beginning with the desired profit, the remodeler determines what level of gross sales at what profit margin is needed to meet this goal. Next he or she assigns individual goals to each person responsible for creating sales. These individual yearly goals are broken down by quarter and then by month. "When the salesperson has an entire month to reach specific goals, the chances are that [he or she] would have several victories within that time period. This accomplishment helps the salesperson's self-esteem. If the goals were broken down more than that, (for instance, into weekly goals) the chances of having no victories within that period would be greater. This situation could adversely affect the salesperson's self-esteem."

The monthly goals would serve as a gauge for the salesperson, telling him or her that sales are off for a month so he or she needs to turn up the heat to make up for the shortfall in the next month.

When developing the individual goals for a salesperson the remodeler needs to keep in mind his or her—

◆ years of experience in the business
◆ time with the company
◆ years of sales experience

Explain Probation Period and Reviews

When a job is offered to a prospective salesperson, the remodeler should describe to the new employee the probation period and the review process. He or she should clearly explain that a review process will help both parties determine if things are working out. These reviews will take place during a 30- to 60-day probation period that should be put into effect. The review process should start at the end of the employee's first week on the job. The review will consist of an interview to judge if the salesperson's expectations of the job were realistic and if the remodeler has communicated his or her expectations clearly.

Another interview at the end of the second and third weeks provides a forum to discuss ideas, ask questions, or seek clarification. These interviews ensure that the salesperson has received no miscommunications and that he or she is performing in a manner that will support the goals of the company. After the salesperson's fourth week on the job the remodeler or sales manager may require meetings only every other week. But the remodeler and the salesperson need to continue the reviews on a regular basis to make sure that each has the same expectations of the job. By taking this initiative, the remodeler greatly lessens his or her chances for disappointment.

Supervise the New Salesperson

After going through the complete interview process, any salesperson who is hired should know what expectations he or she is to meet. But does this mean that the remodeler must tell a salesperson how to do his or her job? Not according to Mathis. "All over America, sales managers are becoming coaches. They don't tell their people how to do their jobs. They just tell them what is expected of them and let them find their own methods. Salespeople must be supported and guided, not directed every step of the way."

One of the appeals of a career in sales is the flexibility of the position. The freedom to move about and call their own shots might be the motivating factor for many salespeople. The remodeler or sales manager would profit from letting successful salespeople use their own techniques to reach their goals.

Train the Salesperson

As in any profession, ongoing training can make a great impact on the success of the individual. Any athlete knows the importance of practice in maintaining top form. The same rules apply in sales. Salespeople must continually seek improvement in order to stay ahead of the competition. Mathis says, "Experts agree that technical knowledge is credited with only 15 percent of a person's success. Therefore, . . . training and continuing education [also must] include basic human relationship skills that will improve their capacity for relating to their prospects."

Technical training can consist of video tapes, books, seminars or specific workshops to demonstrate installation, special applications, or features and benefits of products. "We make sure that we know the latest technology as it applies to the products we carry," says Branstetter. "We watch product videos, listen to seminar tapes, and go to manufacturers' local seminars. Some companies are assigning one of their salespeople to come and work in our showroom. We will be able to observe how they present their products to consumers. That will be extremely helpful." Building human relationship skills is an important part of many companies' training. Tony LaPelusa, of LaPelusa Home Improvements, Inc., in Niles, Illinois, believes that relationship skills are essential. "I believe that every salesperson should go to a Dale Carnegie course on Human Relationships," says LaPelusa. "I've taken it and so has one of my salespeople. It teaches common sense ways to treat people. But it's amazing that so many people don't have the common sense to treat people the way they need to be treated. My philosophy is that the close of the sale starts at the very beginning and that the actual close should be assumed. But basically, all things being equal, it's the salesperson with the best relationship skills that will be the most successful."

Skills such as time management, goal setting, building self-esteem, how to influence people are all topics that can be improved through easily found seminars, tapes, and books.

Conduct Sales Meetings

One of the best ways to keep tabs on the progress of salespeople is through regular sales meetings. These meetings can cover a gamut of topics but should be considered opportunities to provide encouragement, work out problems, congratulate, learn, and celebrate. These times are to brainstorm about the best ways to help salespeople reach their goals—not for admonitions. "In our weekly sales meeting . . ." says Branstetter "we cover a great deal of information, and I feel that it's helpful for us to work together and bounce ideas off of one another." A typical sales meeting might include reviewing the status of previous leads, specific problems with clients, difficult objections, updates on products or pricing, review profit margins on completed projects, production or administrative systems or problems, local industry gossip, or a shift in company goals. "It's rather like raising a child," says Branstetter. "Encouraging and informing is an ongoing but essential process."

For the remodeler who is the owner and salesperson, meeting with a sales or business management consultant once or twice a year may help the remodeler keep the company on target and work out any sales system problems that may have developed in the company.

Motivate the Salesperson

Inevitably, every salesperson will experience sellers slump at some time or other. A remodeler who sees this happening has several ways to deal with it. Phil Rea, president of Phil Rea, Inc., Newport News, Virginia, says, "When some people get real down, they turn to drink or sleep to get over it. I'm lucky. When I get depressed, I get mad. And then all I want to do is work. So that's what I do. I'll start making calls until I sell something and that gets me over my depression fast."

Mark Goldsborough, president of Mitchell, Best, and Goldsborough manages a staff of four salespeople. "When I see one of my people getting into a slump, I try to bring them in the office to talk it through. I'll explain that it happens to everyone and that it will pass if they just keep working. Often I'll have the salesperson . . . go to lunch with one of the more experienced salespeople and talk about how everyone hits [a slump] . . . sometime." Goldsborough also tries to help such a salesperson through the slump as best he can even to the point of going on sales calls with the salesperson. "If I go on a call . . . , I may pick up on something that . . . [person is] doing wrong, perhaps a bad habit they've picked up. Afterward, we can talk it through. Often this solves the problem and the slump is over."

A remodeler who is the primary salesperson of his or her firm has a more difficult time staying motivated because he or she has no one in the office with which to work out sales problems. Attending sales seminars or regular sales training programs will give the remodeler the opportunity to discuss problems, learn new techniques, and brainstorm with other salespeople.

Motivational audiotapes or books may also help to change a

pessimistic attitude. However, if a remodeling salesperson hits a tough period, he or she must remember that this is only temporary. The individual has to find the way that best helps him or her become enthusiastic again. The sales manager can help this process along by being supportive and willing to listen.

Compensate the Salesperson

Remodeling companies probably have as many different ways to compensate salespeople as there are companies. However, certain forms are more popular than others. John Mathis believes that a combination of salary and commission is the most effective. "Having some sort of a salary base helps address a person's basic need for security," says Mathis. "If a salesperson doesn't have this base, [he or she] can become too pushy through desperation and alienate prospective customers. However, the salary should never be enough for the salesperson to live on; 30 to 50 percent of an adequate income should be made up of salary. The rest will be commission. This [arrangement] will ensure that the salesperson remains motivated to sell more."

While remodelers debate the merits of basing a commission on sales price, more and more remodelers are realizing that basing commission on gross profit is more realistic. Branstetter uses a sliding scale to determine the commission percentage. "If the project is sold for a 40 percent margin, the salesperson will receive 25 percent of gross profit. Our minimum margin is 38 percent. If it falls below that, and it's his fault, the salesman doesn't receive a thing. If it's the fault of the production staff, the salesperson still will get paid."

If the remodeler chooses to base the salesperson's compensation on gross profit, he or she must make sure that the salesperson is not penalized by problems in the production department over which he or she has no control. By adding a system of checks and balances, the remodeler can avoid possible dissension between the production and sales departments.

LaPelusa offers his salespeople a base salary plus a commission based on gross sales. Because they are totally responsible for each of their sales, any mistakes affecting the sales price will be reflected in their pay. (See Promote Communication Through Individual Job Management later in this chapter.)

Mark Richardson, vice president of Case Design/Remodeling, Inc., also believes that a base salary is important. Case's salespeople increase their income with a commission based on the gross profit of their collective projects throughout the year. With this system, the commission is evened out across the projects and the salesperson is not penalized as harshly for one job that might have slipped below the acceptable gross profit limit. "Our commission averages out to be between 5 and 6 percent of sales," says Richardson.

Most of the remodelers mentioned above base their commissions on gross profit. However, some companies base it on total volume sold. According to industry expert Linda Case, president of Remodeling Consulting Services, this system has major disadvantages. "In the best of companies, everyone is working together as a team with an eye toward a profitable bottom line. By basing commission on volume, the salesperson may put the emphasis on signing contracts with no regard for profitability. The salesperson can win while the company loses. Secondly, if the salesperson is . . . tied into profitability, [he or she has more] . . . incentive to prepare a comprehensive packet containing all of the information necessary to make an easy handoff to production. Without this detailed information, the production department will . . . run into walls, which can hold up the project and cost the company money."

Because the remodeler who is the owner and sole salesperson really wears many hats, compensation is rarely based directly on sales. While some owners may tie a bonus to their sales success, most take into consideration the many other tasks that they are called upon to perform when setting their compensation.

Promote Communication Through Individual Job Management

Tony LaPelusa has what he calls "the best system in the country!" The major difference between this $1.5 million company and many others is that each salesperson in LaPelusa Home Improvements, Inc., is responsible for everything about the project including taking the incoming lead, selling, estimating, supervising production, and collecting the money for each of his or her jobs. Typically, remodeling salespeople will sell the job, hand it over to the production department, and go on to the next sale. With approximately 200 jobs a year, LaPelusa believes that his method is the best way to ensure follow-through and the quality of his company's final product.

"By having each of us manage our own jobs, we never have to worry about a lack of communication between the salesperson, the production supervisor, and the homeowner," says LaPelusa. "In the traditional method, many details can slip between the cracks. But, [because] the salesperson is totally responsible, if he promises to do something, the chances are much better that this promise will be carried out, and we'll all look better in the eyes of the customer."

In order to best utilize their limited crews, LaPelusa and his two salespeople sit down once a week to schedule their field staff. "This way we all pick the best people for the particular job, and we work it out together. After 29 years in the business, I don't think that this system can be beat."

Action Plan 10—Managing the Sales Function

- Before hiring a salesperson, look to see where your own strengths lie and hire someone who complements, not duplicates, these strengths.
- Create a comprehensive, detailed, written job description or profile.
- List the qualifications that applicants must meet.
- Spend the time to hire the right person for the company; you could be risking a great deal of time and money.
- Use newspaper ads because they are one of the best ways to solicit for employees. Be sure ads are nondiscriminatory and specific enough to draw qualified applicants.
- Use a 15-question interview form with each application to help screen out the least desirable candidates.
- Make face-to-face interviews long enough to get beyond the basics. Prepare a list of open-ended questions that will require the applicant to give longer answers. Ask all candidates the same prepared list of questions.
- Consider using personality profiles or aptitude testing to add a new dimension of information to the process and confirm the gut feeling that you may have about the candidates.
- Don't automatically reject salespeople from another industry. Salespeople who were good in another industry may be good remodeling salespeople.
- Review each new employee at the end of each week for the first month, then every other week for several months. This practice gives each party a chance to clear up misunderstandings and offer additional information.
- Tell the salespeople what goals must be accomplished but not how they must reach the goals. Successful salespeople are creative and love the flexibility of a career in sales.
- Provide ongoing training in sales and personal growth to keep the sales force at the top of their game.
- Use regular sales meetings to maintain control of the team's progress or regular meetings with a sales coach to monitor your own.
- Consider using a combination of salary and commission. Many remodelers believe this combination might be the best for a salesperson's compensation. Salary should be only a third to a half of a living wage.

Chapter 11

Success Stories

Interview with Phil Rea

Company Profile

Business:	Full-line remodeling firm
1991 Annual Volume:	Ranges between $1.5 million and $2 million
Jobs per Year:	200-225
Average Job Size:	$7,800
Personnel:	Salespeople—Owner and one additional salesperson Office Staff—Bookkeeper and receptionist-secretary

Figure 11-1. Phil Rea, president, Phil Rea, Inc., Newport News, Virginia

History

"Even as a child, I knew that I was going to be in sales," says Phil Rea, president of Phil Rea, Inc., "Everyone that knew me told me that. So when I began looking for a job, that's where I looked first."

Phil began his selling career in the automobile industry and rapidly moved up to the sales manager position at a local auto dealership. One day, a salesman who had worked for Phil but had left the dealership stopped in to talk. He mentioned his success in selling foam insulation door-to-door. This idea intrigued Phil, and he went home to discuss with his wife a possible career change.

"We sat down and did the Ben Franklin close," remembers Phil. "We drew a line down the middle of the paper and wrote down the pros and cons of making this change." Since Phil was the top salesperson at the dealership, he could have been gambling a large financial payback. However, after all of the details were written down, the chances for a much larger success were clear. "We weighed the reasons and let the facts make the decision for us."

Within a week Phil was working alongside his former salesperson selling foam insulation. "They wanted me to go into a training pro-

gram for 2 weeks. I said 'No Way! I have to get out there and make some money.'" The manager agreed to skip the training program if Phil would take the time to review the presentation book. By early afternoon on his first day, Phil was knocking on doors.

"On my first appointment that evening, I was giving my presentation to the homeowners. At one point, it calls for the salesperson to remove a heat receptacle [register] and shove a screwdriver up there to feel for insulation. I did that and couldn't find a thing. So I sat back and said, "Mr. Carter, no wonder your heating bills are so high. There's not a stitch of insulation in your walls." Mr. Carter looked at me funny and said, "You damned fool! I'm not supposed to have insulation in an interior wall!" Needless to say, I didn't get the sale. But I also didn't make that mistake again."

After gaining a bit of experience, Phil decided that the best way to learn was to try to sell to the toughest customer available. "So I went right into the richest neighborhood in town. Those people are hard!" This tactic worked and after a month on the job, Phil was the top salesperson in the firm.

Phil left 1½ years later to form a partnership in a specialty remodeling firm. He stayed for 6 months before leaving to form Phil Rea, Inc. After only 2 years in the business, Phil had his own company.

Reasons for Sales Success

Phil says, "I've always been a selling kind of person. I enjoy people and have a keen interest in observing and talking to all kinds of people. One of my favorite things to do is to go to the mall and just observe how people look and how they act. I've always known how to draw others out, and I think that this really works in my favor.

"When I started, I didn't know a thing about construction, so I'd take one of our employees with me as a construction consultant. He'd answer any technical questions. In the meantime he had the chance to see me closing lots of sales. He's now our other salesperson.

"Selling has really changed in the last few years. It's not nearly as structured. There is not the urgency for the close today. It used to be said that 'Be backs aren't greenbacks' meaning that if you had to go back to conclude the sale, chances were really good that you'd already lost the sale. Today, while I still try to close a sale quickly, a second meeting isn't unusual.

"Today, I believe more in building relationships than selling product. [My time] . . . used to be 10 percent presenting the product and 90 percent in the closing portion of the sale. Today, it's just the opposite. I try to bring out the real needs of my prospect. It's not a hard sell at all. In fact, it's so soft that many of my clients don't even realize that they're being sold anything.

"There's still a place for the traditional close in today's sale because people want to be sold. They want you to give them a reason to buy. When you help them, you're both happy.

Figure 11-2. Rea Views on Selling

- Getting out on the street and selling is the best way to learn how to sell.
- Develop a natural interest in people. Learn how to draw them out.
- Spend your time developing a relationship, not trying to close a sale.
- Treat your customers well, like family, if you want them to come back next time.

"We take tremendous pride in the care we take with our clients. We don't really even need any more new clients. We'd have plenty of work if our old clients just kept coming back. But we have to be sure to take good care of them in order to have this happen. We consider Phil Rea customers a part of our business family. Once you do business with us, we assume that you'll do all of your business with us. It hurts to drive by one of our past customers and see someone else doing a job.

"Follow-up is another important part of any sale. After a job is finished, everyone of our clients receives a plant, and then we stay in touch regularly after that. We want to be sure that they are thinking about us."

Advice

Learn by fire. "Get out there and start selling. Don't waste time with a lot of training. Half the stuff you're trying to learn, people don't give a hoot about anyway. Do I know about beams and construction details? Heck no, but that doesn't stop me from being successful selling remodeling. I just work closely with the people who have the technical knowledge. I don't try to do it by myself. Some people wait until all the lights are green before they'll even leave home. This is a waste of valuable time. Trial by error is still the fastest way to learn."

Interview with Mark Richardson

Company Profile

Business:	Design Build Firm
Jobs per Year:	100
Average Job Size:	$80,000
1991 Annual Volume:	$7 million
Personnel:	75 people in two offices— in Bethesda, Maryland, and Falls Church, Virginia.

Figure 11-3. Mark Richardson, vice president, director of design, Case Design/Remodeling, Inc., Bethesda, Maryland

History

After graduating with a professional degree in architecture from Virginia Technological Institute, Mark realized that he most enjoyed the interface between architecture and construction. He joined one of his professors to start a firm that would design and build small remodeling projects—a small version of a design build company. "I found that what I really loved was design and sales," says Mark. "That's what allows me to work so hard. I wanted to deal with this part of the business pie and not as much with the administrative or production [aspects]."

Mark left the partnership in 1980 for a position as a designer-estimator for Case Design/Remodeling, Inc. Rapidly, this position evolved into full-time sales, and within the first 2 years, he was the top salesperson. ". . . one of my keys to success was that I had the design base, which I could apply."

But achieving success was not all easy. As he began his sales career, he had handicaps to overcome. "For the first 5 years, 7 out of 10 prospects would ask me if I was old enough to be selling remodeling," says Mark. "That was frustrating. I grew a mustache but that didn't help enough. I had to build credibility with prospects and wasn't sure how to go about it. So I began to talk above them and interject buzz works and technological jargon. They couldn't understand me, but they quickly got the impression that I knew what I was talking about."

At this point Case Design/Remodeling was based in Washington, D.C. When the firm added an office in Bethesda, Maryland, Mark stayed to manage the administration and sales of the D.C. office. Eventually, the firm consolidated both offices into one large Maryland office. "I'd discovered that I really didn't like the details of administration. In combining offices that responsibility was given to another person, and I could concentrate on design and sales again." For the past several years, Mark has been managing the Bethesda sales department as vice president. The firm also opened an office in Falls Church in 1984.

Reasons for Sales Success

"In order to be a great salesperson you have to be organized. I don't mean that everything has to have its place. I just mean that you have to think organized. I spend 20 minutes every morning getting ready for my day.

First, I'll brainstorm about all of the different things that I'd like to get done. After each activity has been prioritized, I'll estimate the number of minutes that I think it will take to get each done. I compare these minutes with the hours in the day and cut the less important things off the list until the amount of time matches. A 1- or 2-hour contingency time is always included. I use this to take care of those unexpected things that crop up during the day. By writing down my goals for the day, I'm able to visualize exactly what I'd like to get done. This visualization helps me map out my day and gives me a good idea of what's going to happen.

"I try to instill a similar degree of organization in our designers. While I don't require the same sort of lists that I use, I think they can see how well this sort of system works for me and try to emulate it to a certain extent.

"Reaching your sales goals takes the same process that you would use to reach other goals in your life. I . . . [believe] that if I can accomplish the small goals, I can accomplish the larger ones. But it's done step by step. Just like a house is built one stick at a time, so are your long-term goals met one day or week at a time. But I have to start with a vision of my daily goals. The key to this is that you'll never accomplish your goals unless you take them a piece at a time."

The sales staff in this office consists of Mark and four other salespeople, called designers in the Case organization. They meet as a group once a week and each individual designer also will meet with Mark once a week.

The individual meetings are for discussing strategies to reach goals, ways to be more creative in their selling approach, look specifically at monthly, yearly, and weekly goals. "One of the easiest things to do in sales is to waste time. And this will happen unless you have a methodical, structured approach. That's why we work so hard on meeting the strong specific goals of each salesperson."

During the group meeting the designers and Mark discuss general topics such as the status of different jobs, the pulse of the market, company housekeeping details, or problems that one or another might have encountered during the previous week are discussed.

Motivate the Salespeople

When dealing with the ups and downs of his sales staff, Mark looks at them in the same way that he does his customers. "Sales management is basically human relation skills. You have to show your staff that you truly care about them and their problems. The only difference between your staff and your customers is that you have to continue to care about your salespeople every single day. It's not like a customer with whom you will have limited contact. The relationships with your staff can become quite complex. While I'd certainly like them to like me, I'm much more concerned that we respect each other. A healthy dose of respect goes a long way."

All salespeople have ups and downs in their attitudes as well as their sales. "Every one of the Case designers hits seller's slump once in awhile," says Mark. "Until the last few years, when I divvied up the leads, I used to give those in a slump some of the better ones. I felt that this would even things out and make it more fair and give them a chance to sell their way out of the slump. But I've completely changed my attitude about this.

"Now if someone is 'Hot', that's the person who will get the best leads. Their enthusiasm is high and the chances that they will close the sale is much better than the person that's in the slump. When I used to give the best lead to the down person, inevitably they would lose it. Now, while I still give leads to the . . . [salespeople when they are] in a slump, they just don't get the best ones. Just as in baseball, [if they're in a slump], they're not off the team, they're just going to be the relief pitcher, practicing until they work themselves out of their slump. Then they'll be back on the starting team again. I've found that this is working much better, and we're closing more projects. The only time this [policy] isn't the case is when . . . [the lead is] someone's previous client. Then that salesperson gets it no matter what. I truly believe that 90 percent of what a person is buying is the salesperson, and only 10 percent is the company. If the relationship clicked in the past, then it probably will again."

Continue to Educate the Salespeople

Ongoing training is a mainstay of the Case sales department. In-house and outside videos are used to help the sales staff perfect their presentation skills. In addition, Mark works with them closely one-on-one. "Much of any salesperson's success will be created from knowing the basics. They have to constantly review and analyze their approach," says Mark. "We'll sit down and role play. I'll play them and they'll play the customer, and we'll walk through a potentially difficult scenario so that they can see how I would have handled things. This [role playing] is a great way to work on closing, addressing objections, and presenting the company. I can help them by giving the benefit of my experience."

Mark also uses the group sales meeting as a forum for solutions to tricky problems. "If one salesperson is having a problem, chances are that some of the others are too. So I'll ask the other salespeople how they would have handled it. They come up with some very creative answers. Sometimes I learn a better way too. We'll also talk about theoretical strategies that might work in particular situations."

Talking about a salesperson's successes is important too. "Not only does this encourage them, but someone might have an idea that the others could use too. One might have a strategy for how to encourage a customer to

move ahead more quickly. It's very helpful to bring these things up at our meeting. Especially this problem because this point in the sales call is crucial. If we don't keep up the enthusiasm and encourage the customers to commit early in the sales process, the risk of losing them is much greater. The more time passes, the better the chance that the prospect's state of mind will change. This [situation] is what causes the lost sales—a change in the . . . [prospect's] state of mind. So we spend a good deal of time talking about the strategies that might move things along faster."

Stay Flexible

According to Mark, one of the most important factors in remodeling sales success is to remain flexible and creative. "I used to be very rigid about what we'd do, but I've found out that flexibility is better, especially in this market. Right now we're building two shell additions. That's something we never would have done just a couple of years ago. But it's a weird market right now so it's important that you do what you have to do in order to get the business."

Another key is to try to separate Case Design/Remodeling from the pack. "We have to compete in a different arena from our competitors. More than ever before, we're finding that clients are more willing to take risks with quality in order to save money. We have to convince them that . . . [the investment is] worth it to work with us and [that they should] spend the money to do the job right. But in order to do this, we have to be perceived as different from the pack of less professional companies. I compare this to fighting. Why jump in the ring with a 200-pound, highly trained, young boxer when I'm older and not in such great shape? I wouldn't do it. Instead, I'd try to beat him by using my brains not my brawn.

"While most of our competitors jump in and just ask the prospect's what they want done, we'll spend a great deal of time focusing on other issues. We'll start by analyzing their needs, asking lots of questions, finding out what they don't like in their homes currently. We ask questions to find out what's important to them. Right there, we are differentiating ourselves."

Hiring

"When we hire someone, I look at three things: Do they have the basic credentials to do the job? If they do, then I try to determine by the way they present themselves if they have the drive to excel and if they fit in with the vision of the company and the personalities of the other staff members?

"I would consider hiring someone from another industry, but I would have to realize that I'd have to spend a lot of time teaching them about the industry. Even if you've only been in remodeling for a short period, it's amazing how many details you've picked up and are carrying around in your head. Someone from outside the industry would have a lot to learn."

Figure 11-4. Richardson Views on Selling

- In order to be a great salesperson you have to be focused. Plan your day, every day to get the most accomplished. Set specific small goals that will lead to the achievement of your larger goals.
- The key to accomplishing your large goals is to meet it one small goal at a time.
- Sales management is basically human relation skills. You have to show your sales staff that you truly care about them and their problems.
- A salesperson's success depends on his or her mastery of the basics. Therefore, salespeople have to constantly review and analyze their approach to the basics of selling.
- In order to be successful, salespeople must be different and separate themselves from the pack.

Interview with Wanda Chavez

Company Profile

Business:	Design Build Remodeler
Annual volume:	$1.5 million
Jobs per Year:	15
Average Job Size:	$100,000
Personnel:	Owner plus one other salesperson, one secretary, two field employees

History

Wanda began her sales career selling television advertising time for a station that had a mark or two against it: only 2 years old, it was not rated by the national rating firms such as Arbitron. These firm's ratings are the first place a media buyer looks when considering the wisdom of an advertising purchase. On top of this handicap, the small station was competing with much larger Los Angeles stations that covered essentially the same market. But perhaps working with this adversity helped Wanda hone her sales skills to the level at which they are today.

Even though her office was over an hour away from her main prospects and clients, Wanda learned one important lesson from her sales manager. In order to best present the case for the station, the salespeople were trained to always meet the prospects face to face. They were never allowed to mail a proposal to a prospect. "You can't sell from a Fax machine!" was the call of her manager. "This [face-to-face interaction] is a very essential part of the sales process," says Wanda. "Even when I knew that the potential wasn't all that great at that particular moment, I'd make

Figure 11-5. Wanda Chavez, president, Magness Construction, Orange County, California

myself get in the car and drive to meet with them in person. And [because] people tend to buy from people they know and like, this [practice] was an important part of my success."

In addition, selling advertising time taught Wanda the importance of professional business practices.... many salespeople ... don't treat their customers professionally," says Wanda. "Doing simple things such as returning telephone calls promptly and arriving when you say you will can separate you from the crowd. I learned not to drop the ball and to do what I promised to do. In turn, my customers learned that they could count on me."

The tenacity and persistence that Wanda showed finally began to make a difference. "The media buyer would say, 'I've only got $200 to spend. That's too small for you.' In a second, I'd tell them that I'd take it. I figured that any size purchase was my foot in the door. Nothing was too small. I knew that if they tried the station, we'd prove that it would work and they'd be back with something bigger. I was right. This [success] taught me never to give up."

After being rebuffed by a particular advertising agency time and time again, Wanda decided that she had nothing to lose by going directly to the client. Typically, in the advertising business, it's considered extremely bad practice to bypass the advertising agency and go directly to the client. "At that point, I didn't have to worry about hurting a good relationship. I didn't have a relationship at all!" says Wanda. "Once the client heard my story, the [client] . . . insisted that the agency buy some time on my station. This company turned into one of my best clients. I learned that if you want to sell something, go directly to the decision-maker at the top."

Soon she was the number one salesperson, selling more than the other four salespeople combined. After 5 years, she left to go to a larger station in Los Angeles, which meant commuting for over 3 hours each day. Two years later, spending this much time on the road was wearing thin. At this point, Wanda happened to speak to a good friend who owned a handyman service in the Chicago area. "She was doing so well with this service that I started thinking about the possibilities that might exist in my area."

After careful research and planning, she approached one of her advertising clients, a remodeling contractor, with a proposal to open a handyman division for commercial properties and restaurants. She suggested that they market themselves as a one-stop-shopping source for any handyman or maintenance needs in this particular section of the industry. Wanda would be the sole salesperson and responsible for developing business from the ground up. To lessen the risk to the owner, Wanda would be paid purely on commission. John Magness, owner of Magness Construction agreed to give it a shot.

Reasons for Sales Success

"Generating business from a totally new segment wasn't easy. I knew that I would be making a lot of cold calls. Basically, I sat down with the *Yellow Pages* and began calling any restaurant or business chain headquartered in the area. [I called] . . . Wendy's, McDonald's, Circuit City (an electronics chain), and Mrs. Field's Cookies. I knew that if we sold to a multiple location chain, we'd immediately multiply our business."

Their first sale was a job to blacktop and stripe a parking lot for a local McDonald's. "Once again, it didn't matter that this was only a small job, because it got our foot in the door." Once this job was done and done well, that McDonald franchise owner referred them to another who needed his store painted. This lead to a $110,000 restaurant remodel and the division was going strong. Within 4 months Magness Construction was in the process of remodeling four different Wendy's restaurants.

Then John Magness decided to go out on his own. Wanda immediately offered to purchase the company as long as the name, which was established in the marketplace, remained intact. Although Magness relinquished ultimate control, he remained aboard. "John had the construction expertise and I had the sales expertise. We made a great team," says Wanda.

As their business increased, Magness Construction became specialists in restaurant maintenance and remodeling. They could offer expert advice that would make their customer's investment go further. "Restauranteurs work with seating and decorating experts, not contractors. And while these companies can come up with some great ideas, not all of them are feasible when it actually comes time to construct. Once we began to understand the restauranteur's needs, we could suggest that instead of using this expensive surface from ceiling to floor, "Why not substitute a more durable surface on the bottom half. Kicking and bumping won't hurt it, which makes much more sense for places that attract children. Or we could devise a more practical way to place the lighting.' We found that they really appreciated the suggestions. This helped our credibility a great deal."

Once their customers realized that Magness Construction offered residential remodeling as well as the maintenance and handyman services, Magness began attracting home remodeling projects from their commercial clients. This transfer of business became more and more common once the maintenance customers experienced the high level of service that Wanda and Magness Construction brought to the table.

"One of our keys to success is to take pains to pay great attention and take care of every customer. It's much easier to service existing customers well than to beat the streets to find and sell new customers," says Wanda. "Our customers know that if they have a problem, they can call me, and we'll take care of it. They don't have to call twice. This is a pretty rare trait these days and our customers appreciate it."

Cross Industry Selling

"I truly believe that sales skills are transferable from one industry to another," comments Wanda. "The secret is being persistent and servicing the customer. It doesn't matter if you were selling IBM computers or cars, the basics remain the same. You still have to make the clients feel important, as though they are the only customer you have. One of the ways that we show our customers that they matter is to make ourselves totally available to them. We'll write our pager numbers on every contract so that they know that they can reach us 24 hours a day. We take great pride in this."As the success of Magness Construction has shown, the effective sales rules that Wanda learned during her time selling advertising space have been successfully transferred to her remodeling business.

Figure 11-6. Chavez Views on Selling

- Don't take no for an answer. Every no is really a question. It just means that your prospect needs more information about how your product or service will solve his or her problem.
- Don't be afraid to pick up the phone and go right to the top to the real decision-makers.
- Sell face to face. Don't let modern technology remove you from the most effective selling stance. Realize that you cannot sell unless you're right there in front of the prospects to answer their questions and offer the right information to counter objections.
- Pay particular attention to follow-through and professional business practices to overcome the perceived unfavorable reputation of the remodeling contractor.
- Do everything in your power to stick to the schedule. This idea is the key to repeat business.

Notes

Chapter 2. Developing Sales Procedures
1. Tom Hopkins, *How to Master the Art of Selling,*® Warner Books ed. (Scottsdale, Ariz.: Champion Press, 1982), p. 145.

Chapter 4. Gather Information
1. Tom Hopkins, *How to Master the Art of Selling,*® Warner Books ed. (Scottsdale, Ariz.: Champion Press, 1982, p. 44.

Chapter 8. Ask for the Sale
1. Tom Hopkins, *How to Master the Art of Selling,*® Warner Books ed. (Scottsdale, Ariz.: Champion Press, 1982, p. 212.

Selected Bibliography

Estes, Shirley. *Selling Like a Pro*. New York: Berkeley Books, 1988.

Hopkins, Tom. *How to Master the Art of Selling*. Warner Books ed. Scottsdale, Ariz.: Champion Press, 1982.

London, Sheldon I. *How to Comply with Federal Employee Laws*. Washington, D.C.: London Publishing Co., 1991.

Shook, Robert L. *The Perfect Sales Presentation*. New York: Bantam Books, 1986.

Willianhgam, Ron. *Integrity Selling*. New York: Doubleday, 1987.